YOU DID What?!

Audacious Faith Adventures in the Life of

David McCracken

"You Did What?!"
Copyright © 2013 by David McCracken
All rights reserved

Published by David McCracken Ministries
Narre Warren North, Victoria, Australia

Cover Photography and Book Layout by Pete Claproth,
Peter David Creative
Beaconsfield, Victoria, Australia

National Library of Australia Catalouging-in-Publication entry:
McCracken, David
You Did What?! : Audacious Faith Adventures in the
Life of David McCracken / David McCracken
1st edition

Religious
Biography
ISBN: 978-0-9871314-9-2 (pbk.)

All Scripture quotations, unless otherwise indicated,
are taken from the New King James Version®
Copyright © 1982 by Thomas Nelson, Inc.
Used by permission
All rights reserved

One generation shall praise your works to another, and shall declare your mighty acts.

PSALM 145:4

YOU DID *What?!*

DEDICATION

I dedicate this book to my best friend who has selflessly supported me, counselled me, taken bullets for me, has been my constant inspiration and example and without whom this book, and the life it speaks of, would be a dark and gloomy one indeed. I love you **Margaret** more than mortal words can say and never cease to feel a sense of awe that God gave me a partner of such beauty and grace. We have walked together now for over 42 years and the best are yet to come.

Also to my children and grandchildren: **Rachael and Steve, Steve and Sally, Aaron and Tracie, Kirrily, Brianna, Sean, Nathan, Hannah and Liam.** What a blessing each of you are! I am so grateful for all you have taught me over the years.

YOU DID *What?!*

IN GRATITUDE

I am so grateful for the input of many who made this book possible. Among them are:

My parents, **Ernie and May McCracken**, who are now with the Lord. They sacrificed to give my brother and me a start to life that included faithfulness in marriage, diligent hard work, grace at the table, Billy Graham and a God-honouring philosophy in life. I am grateful for their love.

Hilary van Netten, who read and re-read this manuscript and provided so many corrections and adjustments as a proofreader.

Kamal Jassal, who spent many hours and weeks editing and suggesting alternatives that have made the finished work so much better.

Above all else, I thank my ever-faithful **Father** who is not only awesome God but my intimate Dad. He has had to forgive a thousand times and has done so with such love that to serve Him is my joy and delight. He alone gains the glory for this life redeemed and these pages of my journey.

YOU DID What?!

CONTENTS

Chapter	Page	Title
	11	Foreword
	13	Introduction
1	19	Hate-Filled Slab of Pork
2	23	Tobacco, Elvis and Burning Trees
3	31	Terror Upon the Slope!
4	37	No Hands on the Steering Wheel!
5	43	Palm Trees and Molasses Tea
6	51	Wow! I Can Do Anything!
7	59	Ice Cream to Eskimos
8	65	I Discover Adam's Rib
9	73	Fire and Rhetoric
10	77	Joining the 'Marines'
11	87	Stepping on to the Water
12	93	Giving God Grey Hairs
13	101	Seize the Moment
14	107	Tears and Triumph
15	113	Gentle Steel, Elisha and Compassionate Grit
16	121	Claiming Dirt and Dreaming Big
17	127	Values and the Betrayal of Eggs
18	141	Let Out of Prison

Chapter	Page	Title
19	147	Sprinkling Some Salt
20	155	Prophecy and Promise
21	161	Tender Hearts, Steely Resolve
22	167	The Rib Gets Vocal
23	171	Breathing Air on Everest
24	175	The Dark Night of the Soul
25	183	Learning to Die
26	189	No Salary with Abundance
27	197	Burnout and Provision
28	203	Embracing Kangaroos
29	207	A Shock, a Lake and an Irish Jig
30	213	Bacon, Eggs and a New Futura
31	219	Sixteen Lectures a Week
32	223	Lakes and Scenic Walks
33	227	Lions and Hungry People
34	231	No Chewing the Locusts!
35	239	The Lion Roars!
36	245	The Miracle of Avonwood
37	251	Snow in Summer
38	259	Solo No More
39	267	The Road Ahead

YOU DID *What?!*

FOREWORD

David McCracken is a leading apostolic prophet for the 21st century. David, together with his wife Margaret, has pioneered a plethora of things for the Kingdom of God. To my family and our ministries, David has not only been there to give prophetic direction as we move forward in our paths to serve God, he also has been a tower of strength to many. He is courageous and extremely loyal.

In this book you see the life of a courageous man of God who listens and obeys the voice of God. From that ability to hear and willingness to obey, we see through these at times humorous and daring stories, the results of living a life totally surrendered to the will of God. This book isn't just a good read. It has the authority of a life lived which subsequently has authority behind the words of this book. I thoroughly recommend this book and David's ministry to all. You will be empowered, challenged and changed.

My prayer is that people will dare to take the steps of courageous faith that David and Margaret McCracken have displayed throughout this book and in their lives.

Russell Evans
Senior Pastor - Planetshakers City Church, Melbourne, Australia

YOU DID *What?!*

INTRODUCTION

Aaaarrgggh!!!! Without thinking, I simply ran along the branch to its end and jumped off. I ricocheted off branches, ripped clothing, tore skin, screamed and cussed, until I smacked with considerable force into Mother Earth!

Why write my testimony when there are so many desperately needed subjects to write about? Why not a book that teaches, challenges, inspires and instructs people in great Kingdom principles? Why not a book on the prophetic life for which, by God's grace, I have become accepted by so many?

Why write the story of my personal journey?

The truth is that before you declare the message, you must become the message. It is through the God-orchestrated, God-allowed and God-redeemed incidents of one's life that one's life message is forged. The value of the hot rhetoric, the empowered preaching and the inspired prophetic moments come from the fact that they arise out of a heart which has first become the message, before seeking to proclaim it.

Nothing in life is mere accident for one who has settled the fact that their steps have been "ordered by the Lord". As I look back upon my life, with all its laughter, tears, tragedies and triumphs, I realise that God has been forging a message to bring life to others. I write of my journey not as entertainment (though at times I trust you will have a good laugh or two!) but as a declaration of God's grace and as a real-life example of the principles that today I teach to others.

This book is about why I believe what I believe. It is not strictly an autobiography as it leaves out some quite significant seasons in my life. It is about the events that make the message real and touchable. I trust it will educate you in the principles to which a sovereign God has chosen to hold Himself accountable and to which He responds. But I trust even more that it will inspire, encourage and motivate you.

This book contains incidents of my life and my journey that are frank, open, honest and humorous, yet able to be used to bring the reader to a place of being overawed by the wonder, love, faithfulness, forgiveness, long-suffering, generosity, power and sovereignty of my Father.

I want people to have a hunger to know Him more, trust Him more, obey Him more, worship Him more, love Him more, and walk in greater intimacy with His heart as a result of reading this book. My one objective is that you may know Him as I do, love Him as I do and serve Him passionately with total abandonment. And that you may be aided to do so as you read of His amazing grace in the life of one sinner who was, and is, in human terms, so completely ordinary.

I stand today accepted by many as a prophetic voice, yet only those closest to me know of the struggles, the pain, the failures, the mistakes and the human weakness of a very ordinary man who daily stands in wonder at the enormity of God's grace, long-suffering and mercy. Only a few who knew me in the 'early days' know of the crazy stories and ridiculous escapades that must have driven God to laugh, cry and send His rescuing angels time and time again!

And then there are the miracles - the many occasions when God intervened with His miraculous acts of healing, protection, provision and empowerment. As I look back, I am in awe of His incredible faithfulness.

Someone once said to me, "It must take great faith to believe God for miracles like that." No, not really. For me, it would take more faith to disbelieve than to believe! Why? Because of <u>His proven track record</u> where with amazing divine interventions, He stepped into the arena of my life, or family, or ministry and showed us all yet again that His power is without limit and that He can be trusted unquestionably.

During our time together, it is my sincere desire that your heart will be inspired, encouraged and enlarged as you see the wonder and majesty of the Lord we serve together.

Over these 46 years of serving the Lord in various aspects of ministry expression (the last 40 years full-time), I have come to certain unshakeable convictions. The most strongly held of these is that my God is totally predictable in all matters concerning character.

He cannot lie.
He cannot deceive.
He cannot betray.
He cannot mislead.
He cannot misdirect.
He cannot fail!

Why?
Because He is God.

He is the Jehovah of Scripture.
He is the eternally unchangeable One.
He is my Father and yet my Sovereign.
He is my King-Redeemer and yet my closest Friend.

He is totally true.

He is totally pure.
He is totally faithful.
He is totally dependable.
He is total integrity.
He is total diligence.
He is total kindness.
He is total power.
He is total love.

And I have known Him as such for over 49 years, though the first 3 years of which were ones of internal conflict. It is the sole aim of this narrative to reveal Him as such, honour Him as such, and have you experience Him as such.

Am I saying that there have never been times of testing, times of frustration, times of bewilderment, times of pain, times of crying in the night? Absolutely not!

I have known all of those. I have experienced betrayal, church splits, lying accusations, the loss of loved ones, the loss of property, the loss of popularity and acceptance, the seeming death of a ministry, doctors telling me I am all but finished with life, and days of profusely weeping into the carpet! But the one thing I can honestly declare to you is that I have never experienced a single occasion where the Lord has not honoured His Word, and wondrously brought resurrection life out of all of the above.

In this narrative, I want to talk openly about this wonderful covenant-keeping Lord of my heart. I want to share with you the absolute confidence that you can rightfully have in His abundant heart toward those who walk according to His Word. By His Word, I refer to not only His written Word, the Bible (which is the non-negotiable foundation), but also His intimate word to our hearts that daily direct our ways.

As you are reading, you will discover some of the true-life tales of mine which at times are an open window into the inner struggles I experienced, and at times a blast of Irish wit and humour! I have no doubt some of you may consider I am grossly exaggerating points here and there. But let me assure you, other than a little 'poetic liberty' when describing certain disaster-ridden, funny events, that is simply not the case. I have taken great pains to subject this narrative to those who were privy to the facts at the time, and who are good enough friends to be mercilessly honest in their appraisal.

Why have I named it "You Did What?!"?

I humbly suggest that you will have that question more than adequately answered as you read, and you may well use that phrase a few times yourself as you now venture on my journey.

David

YOU DID *What?!*

Chapter One

HATE-FILLED SLAB OF PORK

I was born into a God-fearing Irish home in Newcastle County Down, Northern Ireland, with wonderful parents. I was given a Bible to read as soon as my prowess with the English language had progressed beyond the "da-da, goo-goo" stage.

We moved to England when I was 18 months old and lived there for some 6½ years. My brother Tony (2½ years older) and I were the best of friends and he was the best of older brothers to me in every way.

When living for a short while in the high country on the border of Wales, we snow tobogganed to school together, caught rabbits with ferrets, watched Dad shovel a way down to our front door because of heavy snow falls and protected one another from hostiles, real and imagined.

In Essex, where we also lived for a while, there was a disused show-ground on the Village Common. One day, while strolling through it, a gang of young thugs leapt out of one of the large show tents and grabbed Tony. I managed to get away and ran for home.

Mum was the cook on a large estate and we lived in a wing of the huge manor. Upon hearing my declaration, "They're gonna kill Tony!", my mother leapt into action like the proverbial lioness protecting her cubs! She grabbed some lethal looking utensil from the kitchen, whistled up the two huge dogs that protected the estate, and ran like an Olympian to the show-ground.

As we burst into the tent, the scene was one of terrified young boys being humiliated and tormented by the gang of thugs (we called them 'Bodgies' in those days). Mum unleashed the dogs with orders to attack, and then hurled herself into the gang flailing at them with that gigantic cooking utensil. Chaos!

By the time the local policeman got there on his bicycle, it was the Bodgies who needed rescuing, not my brother!

Mum was our hero.

Right through our childhood years, Tony and I would speak in awe of her ability to do the impossible and adapt to whatever the situation demanded.

Mum was a <u>pioneer in spirit</u>. She was a throwback to the days when a generation worked hard and considered life a privilege. She would have been right at home going to the river to get the water supply, digging the earth to plant the crop and fighting off wild Indians while doing so.

It is sad that very few of today's generation possess the pioneering spirit. Just imagine the incredible potential that could be unleashed from within all of us if we were less of the settler and more of the pioneer. Can I encourage you to rediscover that perspective on life and begin to take those horizons others merely dream about?

In 1955, my parents migrated to New Zealand to give my brother and myself every opportunity for a positive future. Dad, ever looking for new things to try, had a go at accountancy (he was highly qualified as such), sheep farming ("If my ancestors can do it, so can I."), dairy farming ("How hard can it be to get milk from a cow?"), pig farming ("Even easier as you don't have to milk them!"), and breaking in native bush land ("All you need is a slasher and some sweat."). When Dad decided to go into pig farming mixed with dairy farming (at the same time on the same property!), we worked from dawn to dusk and no one harder than Mum. She seemed invincible.

One day, a large (and notably vicious) sow was endangering her piglets. Without a word, Mum climbed over the fence and went in to the rescue. With a piglet under each arm, she raced back across the paddock with an enraged, hate-filled slab of pork inches behind her.

It is amazing what adrenalin can do!

Without time to climb the fence, Mum simply cleared it like a hurdle! And did it with a screaming piglet under each arm! To this day, none of us can figure out how that was even humanly possible. Faith is a bit like that. Maybe we need to imagine a 500kg porker behind us and start believing that our supernatural Adrenalin-Giver can empower us to clear the fence!

Of this I am certain: we are capable of doing so many more things in life than most of us settle for. Rediscover your pioneering spirit!

YOU DID What?!

As Dad continued to shift a lot, Tony and I depended on each other for friendship. He was then, and is now, a brother I love and treasure.

Chapter Two

TOBACCO, ELVIS AND BURNING TREES

As I drew near to adolescence, I remember well Dad's determination for us to get 'saved'. Although often struggling with his own spirituality and inner restlessness, Dad resolved that we would all get to know Jesus and honour Him. A staunch, old-time Wesleyan Methodist, he fervently believed in the need for us to 'get right with God'.

It was a great joy, many years later, for me (then a pastor) to baptise Dad on the same day as my son, Steve. My Dad and my son, one after the other, honoured the Lord that day. That was one of God's wonderful bonus moments.

YOU DID What?!

Back to my adolescent days...

I was taken to church, Billy Graham crusades and tent meetings, and subjected to years of persistent evangelising. However, I was made of stronger stuff.

Just after entering teenage years, I remember standing behind a door in my auntie's house listening to her explode to my father, "Ernie! Ernie! You have two sons. How is it possible that all the good has gone into one and all the bad into the other??!!"

I certainly didn't need divine revelation to know which one I was! My brother Tony was, and is to this day, a kind, gentle, selfless and altogether caring person who is incredibly easy to love by all who truly know him. (My auntie was actually a wonderful person and I loved her dearly but, on this occasion, had simply pushed her too far.)

My childhood and younger teenage years were spent gaining the wrath of teachers, defying my coach in national athletics, damming up a river so that it flooded the main road and disrupted traffic, shooting at cows in a neighbour's cowshed with an air gun during milking time, smoking an original blend of tobacco and rope and dried tea and paying for it, some awesome fights worthy of my Irish ancestry, worshipping Elvis, and being convinced that I was quite easily the most wonderful person I had ever met!

My ego was monumental, my humility undiscovered, my desire to do the daring quite scary, and my conviction that I was indestructible unshakeable.

During that time, I had a very close friend whose father was the farm manager on a large property.

On one occasion, we arrived at his home after dark, and upon entering the house, I said very sincerely to his father, "Is there anything we can possibly do to help you on any of the major projects that you are facing?" With humour tinged with sarcasm, he said, "Well yes, there is. You know those large trees that run down the centre of the property, why don't you boys remove them for me before supper!"

My offer had been sincere, and now my wrath was just as sincere! The trees he had mentioned were huge, and you could see them for miles as they towered over the landscape.

I pulled my friend aside and declared, "Enough is enough! Your father must be taught a severe lesson." We then proceeded to the tractor shed and took matches, one large container of petrol each and several newspapers tucked under our arms. I instructed him to go down to one end of the line of trees and I would proceed to the other end of that line of trees. We would then arrange the newspapers, thoroughly douse all the branches we could reach with petrol, back off to a respectable distance and then hurl something in to ignite them! Remember that it was pitch black!

As I was stumbling my way across the paddocks in the dark, I had a brilliant brainwave and remembered that halfway down the line of trees, there was a particularly tall one which really stood out. I reasoned that if I could climb toward the top of it and set the tip of it on fire, it would look like a huge candle that would be seen for miles!

The climb was very difficult and took a considerable amount of time as I was carrying newspapers and matches. I had decided that I could not carry the can of petrol. Eventually I reached where I had been aiming for and began to arrange the paper around the trunk of the tree. At the same time, I was working out my swiftest escape route down. This was going to be an awesome sight, and I could not wait to see the impact it would have on my friend's father!

Finally ready, I positioned myself to strike the match. But suddenly, I realised that I could already smell smoke and that it was coming from the tree I happened to be in!

My friend had had the same brainwave as I did, but his was to light the fire at the bottom of the tree! He had saturated branches in petrol and thrown in the match! Aaaarrgggh!!!! Without thinking, I simply ran along the branch to its end and jumped off. I ricocheted off branches, ripped clothing, tore skin, screamed and cussed, until I smacked with considerable force into Mother Earth!

There is, of course, more to this story but I have chosen to blank it out of my memory bank as it is altogether too painful. Besides, I think you have the general idea.

On another occasion, Tony and I decided we would canoe around the edge of Lake Rotorua. We figured with both of us paddling in the same canoe, we would do it in a couple of hours max. We set out early one Saturday morning with the somewhat anxious concern of our parents. The trip took almost two days and we didn't return until late on the Sunday night!

We got caught in a storm, nearly sank, had the canoe nearly disintegrate as we paddled too close to an underground hot spring that causes the water to boil, and hardly slept a wink overnight. It took weeks for our muscles not to ache, but what a great memory!

As I look back on my childhood and its many escapades, I realise how tame and predictable adult life can become if we let it. I firmly believe that those of us serving the Lord need more of the spirit of adventure and daring if we want to live life as God intends it. In our attempts to be more responsibly-minded, let us also be sure to keep the conquest spirit alive!

Well, there you have it - the briefest of glimpses into my childhood, living beyond the reach of God's control. I eventually held out until the age of sixteen.

But something I learnt then and still marvel at today is the **persistency of God's love.**

As I began to experience the realities of life at the age of sixteen, I realised the incredible potential for disaster that lay like a crouching tiger within me, and surrendered my life's control to Jesus Christ. What a transformation! I was a new creation! I witnessed to family and friends and had the joy of leading several to the Lord and His wonderful love.

But the honeymoon lasted only a few power-packed months.

It was then that I discovered I had a vicious and determined demonic adversary dedicated to destroying me and that he was the master of deception. He persuaded me that nothing had fundamentally changed and that I was still the same person. It is obvious to me now that the theology of those around me at that time did not help as it emphasised continually the need for 'change' if I was ever going to serve God acceptably. The thought of being His fully accepted son and already complete in Christ, was not mentioned.

In addition, I had a brain that had been programmed for years to believe that if something was going to be achieved, it had to be done by the sweat and diligence of my own hard work.

I loved the salvation the Lord had given me. I was thrilled at the provisions and promises He granted, and the newfound Christian community was great! However, the simplicity of accepting that I was an entirely new person and that I could now trust the Holy Spirit 100% to guide me and empower me for life, was a major challenge to me.

More and more I began to make my own decisions, and less and less I prayed with any real sense of need or fervency. I was still determined to live a successful Christian life that honoured the Lord, but through confidence in my own diligent, aggressive approach to life. I had mistaken religious commitment of the will with true spirituality, and those looking on at my zeal for church activities also mistook one for the other. They would have termed me a 'zealot' for the Lord.

However, zeal for the Lord's work has always been shared between those who are obediently outworking His daily directives, and with those who do not know Him intimately nor even listen to His voice consistently, but know how to do the 'church' thing really well. It is so easy to equate such aggressive diligence to the 'cause' with true spirituality, but it is not always the case. Progressively, my dependence on the Holy Spirit and His supernatural grace decreased and my dependence on iron-willed Irishness increased.

Oh, what folly! Such an invitation is not ignored by the adversary of our souls. I began to lose battles with temptation, and condemnation and confusion became my constant companions. Why could I not succeed? I still loved God but apparently had no power to live for Him.

Those who knew me saw the outward display of a Christian mask, but failed to detect the decay that had set within me. How desperately we need to be more spiritually sensitive to people and to their inner struggles. It is not something that will always come naturally and for most of us, it will require us diligently asking God for it and pursuing it in prayer.

There comes a time when condemnation and a deep sense of inner failure become greater adversaries than the sin that originated those feelings.

Finally I accepted my defeat and began three years of wilderness wanderings. Never having possessed the ability to do things half-heartedly, my condemnation, anger and pain drove me to become what could be described as a 'dedicated backslider'!

Those were three ugly, self-focussed, never satisfied, morally weak, painfully empty years of knowing how much I missed my friendship with the Lord, and yet living a life which must have hurt and offended Him constantly.

But oh, the amazing persistence of God's love! Little did I know that a lady in the Baptist church I had attended had been given a divine commission. God's instructions to her were, *"Pray every morning and every night for that young man until he breaks and comes to his senses!"* Day after day, week after week, month after month, year after year, she prayed and prayed and prayed, with absolutely no encouragement from me!

(Dear Reader, never underestimate the power of faith-filled, enduring prayer. If you are battling discouragement after years of pursuing a loved one for Christ, here is the word of the Lord to you: *"Never give up!"*)

Finally, after three miserable and self-willed years, the Lord put aside the gentle persuasion method and got Himself some heavy artillery!

It was time for God's bazooka!

Chapter Three

TERROR UPON THE SLOPE!

I was invincible!

As I stood looking at that steep, snow-covered mountain slope before me, with toboggan in hand and ready to launch, that is exactly how I felt.

Watching on were a goodly number of fear-filled, lesser mortals who could not believe the action I was about to take.

But, let us backtrack for a moment…

In my backslidden state, I still had this hope that somehow God could still reach me.

Oh, how I love Him for His incredible, persistent, pursuing love! You can run to the ends of the earth (as the Psalmist puts it), but you will still find Him there. Even with all of my self-will and sinfulness, deep down inside I had retained a love for Him. I know it sounds ridiculous, but like so many, it was my inability to live the Christian life successfully which had me running, not because I had ever stopped loving my Saviour.

After my first hundred or so defeats, I backslid because it became too painful to anticipate another failure. And so I fled, not from Him, but from the reality of my own failures. I chose to live a make-believe life of flamboyant irresponsibility in the daytime and a torment-controlled one at night. My greatest anguish of soul was that I knew the truth but had no faith to live it. Yet deep down, beyond the gaze of mortal man, there was still a flicker of hope that one day God would rescue me. It was this small spark that He saw.

Any mortal would have given up on me and proclaimed me a write-off. But not my King! It is so easy to love Him with abandon now as I remember His love for me then. But, as I was about to discover, love can be 'tough'!

It was so subtle and cunning, but oh, so effective! The Baptist youth were going on a ski trip to Mt. Ruapehu and offered to take me along free of charge (obviously they were hoping to re-evangelise me). I couldn't resist.

We arrived and they fitted me with some skis. But after a few moments of witnessing my awesome capacity to violently connect with children and grannies alike, they swapped my skis for a toboggan. I looked hard for a slope that was halfway worthy of a red-blooded young Irishman, and there it was - the perfect invitation. It loomed as a large sign which yelled out, "Beware!!" "Dangerous!!" "Do not approach this slope!!" Outstanding! It had glory written all over it!

So, here is where we started this narrative...

I was invincible!

As I stood looking at that steep, snow-covered mountain slope before me, with toboggan in hand and ready to launch, that is exactly how I felt.

Watching on were a goodly number of fear-filled, lesser mortals who could not believe the action I was about to take. I hurled myself forward, head first upon the toboggan, skilfully using my feet as both rudder and brakes. It was breathtaking! Caution evaporated and speed increased as I flew down the slope only feet away from the edge of an incredibly steep (almost straight down!) descent into the valley below.

I was loving it! Right up until the moment I hit that bump. It was such a very small, insignificant bump. But I learnt something that day - at the right speed, a little bump can take you a very long way!

Before I could gasp a breath, toboggan and yours truly were airborne! My feet were flailing hopelessly in mid-air as I endeavoured to use them as brakes. With one vicious bounce to the left, we hurtled together off the edge! My previously most rapid pace was now an uncontrolled blur of blinding white.

And what, you may ask, was I doing as I screamed my way into the history books? I was repenting! Oh, how I repented!! Then I volunteered. I volunteered for Africa! I volunteered for China! I volunteered for Mars and the moon! "Dear God, if I survive this, I am Yours!"

Then I saw this blur of something immediately ahead. I yanked the toboggan out from under me and somehow managed to put it before me as a battering ram. Together we sliced through the 'blur' like a knife through butter. That 'blur' was a crowd of people, including some of the Baptists! I scattered good God-fearing Baptists to the left and right but only then did I realise where they had been sitting - in front of a huge hunk of granite!!

Toboggan first and me second, we slammed into the granite! There I was, my left side mangled, just flopping all over the place, and blood dramatically pumping from the left side of my cranium. An Englishman, with a 'Terry Thomas' moustache that you could fly with, stood in front of me, and his next words were immortal. "Oh, I saaay, are you all right?" **All right??!! Are you kidding??!!**

I had several days in the Waikato hospital becoming 'all right'. They were days to contemplate, days in which I came to a lifetime conclusion - living life with me at the controls was outright dangerous! What years of preaching failed to achieve, that toboggan ride did in a few seconds.

As I recommitted my life and future into God's hands, I was overwhelmed that He would still accept me. But He did. My sincere and heartfelt repentance was met with what I now know to be His absolutely predictable response, which is His loving Father's heart. Those ten days in hospital were an excellent opportunity to cement those new commitments into a more intelligent rededication of my life to the Great Creator of snow-covered mountains!

Oh, by the way, should you ever have the urge to live life your own way and independent of His directives, I have some spine-chilling news for you. In Heaven's great garage in the skies, God has millions of toboggans! And one of them has your name on it. He simply loves you that much. Happy little thought, isn't it?

So ... did it have to be that way? Did I have to go through those three years of soul-destroying darkness? If not, then what was I missing? What was so wrong with the fervent, hard-working, slugging-it-out philosophy with which I had begun my Christian journey? I really had tried so hard. Every possible religious endeavour had been pursued. That, of course, was the problem. **I** had tried so hard. And **I** had failed.

The choice is simple: we either strive to live this Christian life with human frailty; or we live life through supernatural empowerment out of intimacy with Father's heart.

Friends, there really is a better way.

Living through "Supernatural Empowerment"

YOU DID What?!

Chapter Four

NO HANDS ON THE STEERING WHEEL!

So a new life had begun, but where would I find the strength to succeed where I had previously failed?

My job had taken me to Hamilton and I needed to find accommodation. There was only one door open, and that was with a man and his family who attended a Baptist church where he was a deacon.

Basil Hanson was different from any other Christian I had met up until that time. He seemed to radiate life and goodwill. Serving the Lord did not seem a difficult thing for him. He did it with a passion, which he invariably surrounded with fun and a wonderful sense of humour.

Through Basil, I was introduced to a group who had just launched a coffee house with a difference. This drop-in centre was run by a group of young people who totally amazed me with their sincerity and enthusiasm. They had a 'commission' from the Lord to witness about the redeeming power of Jesus to bikie gangs, drug addicts and others who had been caught up in the harsher realities of life.

Those were the beginnings of 'Teen Challenge' in New Zealand. Teen Challenge had just been launched by David Wilkerson in USA as a result of his work with inner city gangs such as the notorious 'Mau-Maus'. His book came out some years later and became a worldwide best seller called "The Cross and the Switchblade". The book was later made into a successful movie, starring Pat Boone and Erik Estrada.

As I questioned Basil and the team at Teen Challenge and listened to awe-inspiring testimonies from converted gang members now empowered as radiant Christians, I hungered for what they had discovered.

They told me of 'the baptism of the Holy Spirit', which Jesus had promised to send when He left His disciples. I discovered such Scriptures as Acts 1:8 *You shall receive power when the Holy Spirit comes upon you.* I heard about 'speaking in heavenly languages'; and that miraculous healings were for today, and not just in Bible times.

I could see in them the evidence of what they said; and with diligence, read and re-read many Scriptures on the subject. It was so very clear as I read verse after verse! How was it possible I had never seen this before?

Then came that wonderful day when Basil prayed for me and I received the empowering of the Holy Spirit. Although I did not speak in other tongues immediately, I most certainly did feel totally different. My intimacy with God increased, as did my zeal for prayer and witnessing to others. I began to see my Christian life not as a gritting of the teeth to do right, but an exciting journey in which His Holy Spirit was there daily to guide me and empower me.

However, there was still one thing lacking, as I had not yet begun speaking in tongues (God's promised gift of a heavenly prayer language).

It happened like this. A friend and I had been over to Tauranga to attend some meetings being run by a minister called Des Short. In those meetings, we discovered corporate worship which was incredible. We had never seen anything like it! People were totally lost in their love and passion for Jesus, and would stand for hours singing and praying for one another.

Driving back to Hamilton, we were buzzing. After singing non-stop for hours at the top of our voices, we had none left with which to speak. As we travelled on in silence, my companion (whose voice was as hoarse and worn out as my own) suddenly began to sing in the most beautiful, clear voice as she worshipped the Lord. You could feel God's presence fill the car!

I will NEVER forget the following moments! We were hurtling down a long hill when I suddenly felt this surge of love and emotion whelm up inside of me towards the Lord. It felt like a river had been uncorked!

As I opened my mouth to sing, what came out was a language I had never heard before. I was so stunned that I momentarily forgot the car, and both hands shot to the ceiling in adoration and praise!

Fortunately, God must have had an angel or two on duty, and the car kept right on course until a scream from my passenger brought me back to reality!

From that moment on to Hamilton, we sang and spoke in our new languages. And I still do to this very day.

It would be misleading to suggest that from then on my Christian life was easy. As you will read in later chapters, that simply was not so. However, it would be true to say that I felt an empowerment to live; and a hunger and an understanding of the Scriptures that were far beyond what I had experienced in my earlier attempts to live the Christian life. Oh, how the Bible started to come alive to me from that moment on!

Perhaps the most wonderful aspect of this season for me personally, was the revelation that I now had supernatural help to live a spiritually empowered life. Failure was no longer a predictable and inevitable outcome.

I still had to choose. I still had to make right decisions. I still had to live with spiritual disciplines. But at least now my faith was emboldened by the knowledge that the Person of the Holy Spirit was released in a greater measure to help me, as those right choices were made.

As the Holy Spirit talked to me and showed me Scriptures I had never realised were there, I discovered the most powerful truth of how complete and total was the redemption that Jesus bought for me on that cross. I saw that the Christian life was not a religious endeavour to please God, but a wonderful relationship with Him.

I discovered that even when I failed, He loved me because He is my Father. I discovered that I could not 'earn' His love by striving to be better.

I discovered that through the sacrifice of Jesus, Father already loves and accepts us unconditionally as His adopted sons and daughters.

It is impossible to destroy that love. We are fully loved and fully accepted. If we could only get a revelation of that, we would run to give Him what He desires more than any other - our love and affection.

We are talking about the power of intimacy, a true friendship with God. And, through that relationship of intimacy and closeness to His heart, being able to hear His voice clearly and have a love-passion to do what He says.

In those earlier years of trying to be righteous and pleasing to God, I did not know then what I do now. True spirituality was never designed by God to be an external restraint, applied by the gritting of one's teeth in determined obedience to the 'cause'. It was designed to be a well of life springing up from within! = Water gushing out. Bursting. Wall Fall.

True righteousness is the life of Christ (in the Person of the Holy Spirit) unlocked and flowing freely from within us, and which is made possible by the uncluttered devotion of our hearts. I am talking of a passionate desire to please Him, which comes not out of fear or persuasion, but out of love and desire! We then pursue the most noble of goals being that every attitude, every conversation, every deed and action will bring Him honour and pleasure.

Friends, as we are bringing pleasure to Father's heart, His heart's automatic response is to bestow His love and miraculous favour upon us. It is called His *grace* [which literally means 'undeserved favour, gift or ability for a task']. We can experience the knowing that *our steps are not only ordered by the Lord* [see Psalm 37:23] but will also be daily sustained by Him. We need that more than any other singular thing on this planet.

> His grace will bring security to our hearts.
> His grace will bring peace to troubled waters.
> His grace will bring fruitfulness to our ministries.
> His grace will bring reconciliation to our family life.

His grace will bring success to our business life.
His grace will bring His divine interventions against those forces which are arrayed against us.

I have discovered that God can do more with a flick of His fingers than all our human striving will achieve in a lifetime. When I now go into battle, I thank the Lord I can do so knowing that I am not dependent upon my human ability, but rather on His Omnipotent power unleashed on my behalf in the Person of the Holy Spirit.

What an awesome thought!

Chapter Five

PALM TREES AND MOLASSES TEA

After discovering Teen Challenge and receiving the baptism of the Holy Spirit, I wanted to share my new found faith in Christ with as many as possible. Friday nights were spent down at the Teen Challenge Centre talking with street kids, bikies, derelicts, and even some church people who desperately needed to know God.

It was during this time that I heard of another new organisation which provided involvement for Christian youth. It was called 'Youth with a Mission' or YWAM. Upon hearing that they wanted young people to sign up for a missionary trip to Fiji, I immediately volunteered. After some basic training and initiating in local evangelism in Hamilton, we were ready to go to Fiji for 5 weeks. Little did I know that I would stay on there for 3 months.

Fiji was a time of great faith, harvesting and even ministry development, but most of all it was a time of learning.

It was my first taste of teamwork and walking according to the 'rules'. We had all sorts of rules - rules to do with attitudes, conduct, speech, but the one I found the most difficult was the dress code. Here we were in the middle of Fiji wearing long-sleeved shirts, ties and long trousers while the Pacific sun pounded down at noonday. It was in those days that God really challenged my motives and my attitudes. Why was I really here? To feel comfortable; or to win souls for Christ amongst a people who, in that generation, expected missionaries to dress that way? I feel like asking the same question today of those who grumble and complain about having to consider their brother in some area of personal restraint in order to not be a stumbling block.

Another thing God worked on was our humility. And, when doing so, He certainly knew how to set us up!

One of the young ladies on the trip was an Anglican. We, who were of a Pentecostal flavour, decided we had better help her as best as we could so that she wouldn't struggle too much with praying for the sick, etc. Poor girl!

We did, of course, endeavour to show her by example. We prayed for hours, we screamed at demons, and roared with authority at people who had head colds. We were the empowered ones! We trusted she didn't take too much notice of the fact that not too many of those we prayed for were actually healed or even impressed with our enormous spirituality. At least we had the formula right and that alone was worthy of her attention.

Then one day, when we were taking a break for lunch, she looked heavenward and began to talk with someone. What on earth was she doing? And at lunch time!?! She then informed us that Father had told her to go to Labasa Hospital, and to pray for certain ones who were sick there. Poor girl! We volunteered to go with her. She quite obviously was going to need us when met with such significant disappointment.

She entered the hospital with us brave Pentecostal warriors in tow ready to bail her out when it became necessary. We came to the very first ward and she completely ignored it! "How does she expect people to get healed if she doesn't at least go through the motions?", we wondered. "Has she not even read the manual? Poor girl!" To our increased consternation, she ignored the second ward also.

And then she did that heavenward thing again. We heard "Okay, Father", and she turned into this particular ward which only had a handful of people in it. "Doesn't she know anything about the law of averages where the more people you pray for, the higher your chances of getting at least one of them healed? Poor girl!"

But it was about then that Father must have started to really enjoy Himself. With a simple, gentle statement and not even a trace of a good Pentecostal roar, she informed the first one that they were healed and could now get out of bed! As we pinched each other to ensure this was not an illusion, the patient did exactly as she instructed and walked out of the ward grinning like a Cheshire cat! Our 'poor girl' proceeded to then pray for each one there with exactly the same result. And she accomplished all of this without even knowing the 17 laws of divine healing by Itoo Kinhav Ahmega Mini Stree. Poor girl!

While wiping away a combination of bewilderment and envy, we came to the realisation that the Lord was not so interested in our formulas or claim to heritage, but in the state of our hearts. We learnt a valuable lesson that day concerning the value and esteem that we should show one another and the true mockery of pride.

We also discovered that one experience is worth a truckload of knowledge. We learnt that when our Anglican friend had received the call to go on this YWAM trip, she had been lying in hospital partially paralysed due to an accident, and that Jesus had miraculously walked into her ward and healed her. No wonder she had faith. I think we had all been the subject of a heavenly con! We also learnt that it is not how many you pray for but how intimately you hear His voice. 'Poor girl's' heavenward thing had spoken to us all!

From then on things got better and we began to see people get both saved and healed. During a time when a few of us were assigned to a small valley area which contained several villages, we saw over 300 people come to Christ. The hunger of the people to know reality truly touched our hearts and we so rejoiced as they burst out smiling when first feeling the touch of Father's love for them. We filled our days with walking tracks, witnessing, praying for people and having team discussions, and would then collapse to sleep at night.

And then there was the 'tea'. It was the custom that whenever we entered a house in one of the villages, we were offered a large stainless steel bowl of tea. This tea had been brewed with sugar and milk and then brewed again. And then it was brewed and brewed and brewed and brewed some more. It was the closest thing to molasses I have ever had to drink. The trouble was that, being zealous for the 'cause', we visited house after house after house after house!

The day became a challenge between a dedication to witness to as many as possible, and the very real possibility that we would either pass out or drown internally from the effects of so much hospitality! And then there was the lack of public toilets! Why did we drink the tea, you may ask? Because we learnt that in their culture, tea was the mark of hospitality and us drinking it was the mark of our respect.

When returning from yet another glorious day of muddy trail-walking, mosquito-swatting, body-sweating and tea-drowning witnessing for Jesus, I was reminded of how annoyed one could get back home if one had to walk too far across the car park to get into church, only to find that someone else had taken one's favourite pew.

The Fiji chapter would not be complete if I did not mention the coconuts. Oh, not only that they were great for the thirst and we enjoyed the crunch of the coconut flesh itself, but I remember them well for quite a different reason.

We had gone into this village that had a resident witch doctor type person who felt the area was all his. He deeply resented us being there and made it known. Well, to a red-blooded young Irish man filled with power from on high, that was like the throwing down of a challenge. And one that had to be answered. I summoned my interpreter (a wonderful Fijian-Indian Christian named Nathan Gaunda) and walked into the 'doctor's' hut.

Upon my sharing the gospel with him, he became irate and began to blaspheme and say derogatory things about the God we served. Now you have to bear in mind, that although I was at this stage redeemed and filled with the Holy Spirit, I was young in the sanctification process and my Irishness was still very much alive. I became annoyed and then I became REALLY annoyed.

As I looked around his hut, I saw the coconuts and I immediately thought of the story of Elijah calling fire out of Heaven [story account in 1 Kings 18]. Now in the full stride of heated emotion, I slammed one coconut in front of the 'doctor' and the other one in front of Nathan and myself. Then, with great theatrical flair, I picked up a large machete lying on the floor and announced that his god should dry up his coconut and my God would dry up my coconut! And then, through Nathan, I told him that if my God did not dry up my coconut, he could take our heads off with the machete. Nathan's eyes flashed with disbelief as he shook his head and refused to pass on the message! However, something in my own eyes told him it wasn't up for debate and he passed it on. Well, the 'doctor' stared, and then violently leapt to his feet screaming and ran out of the hut!

To this very day, I have no idea what would have really happened. But I have a sneaking suspicion that, after He had got over the shock, God would have actually dried up that coconut. If for no other reason, God would have done it to stand by the heart of one who was standing for Him, and whose irresponsible and undisciplined outburst was the fruit of devotion to Him. It is my personal persuasion that the angels were also cheering rather non-religiously on that day! I think it a pity that sometimes, in our pursuit of propriety, we would rather be judged as acceptable at the Vicar's tea party, than provoke the explosive approval of angels armed for war.

Then there was the railway bridge.

It was one of those days where you did not want to quit. It had been incredibly rewarding but now the sun was setting and fatigue was settling in. In addition, we had totally miscalculated our time of walking back to the village and it was now dark. We realised that the normal way back was going to take us a very long time.

As we stopped to consider our energy levels, a team member remembered a risky shortcut. It was an old derelict railway bridge that stretched over a deep ravine. It had sleepers missing and gaps where decay had made its mark. In broad daylight it would have been extremely risky, but in utter darkness, it was suicidal to even contemplate it. But then someone reminded us of the Scripture, *The steps of a good person are ordered by the Lord* [see Psalm 37:23a]. We decided to claim it quite literally, and proceeded to walk across the bridge in that pitch black condition! To this day, I do not know how many angels were involved in keeping our feet on those disintegrating sleepers, but we ALL made it to the other side!

As I sit here and look back on some of those crazy things we did when we were young, I realise how much we tested the grace of God. But I also feel that He enjoyed the entertainment, and got a buzz out of the rawness of our faith and trust. In fact, I think He could do with a little more of that today.

So, on one hand, God humbled us during that Fijian summer, and yet on the other, He emboldened our hearts. He taught us sensitivity to the customs of those we witnessed to, while provoking us to take stands of authority. We discovered that a sweat-stained shirt and muddy feet could be things of honour. There was no satisfaction quite like that of nightly collapsing exhausted, knowing you had led a soul out of darkness into the embrace of Father's love.

Those were the good days. They were days of simplicity; of learning to hear and learning to obey. For decades to come, I would miss those days.

YOU DID What?!

Chapter Six

WOW!
I CAN DO
ANYTHING!

So here stood the new me: passionately in love with Jesus, empowered by His miraculous Holy Spirit and enough zeal to power up New York!

However, it would also be true to say that I knew absolutely nothing about what I was supposed to live like and why. I was empowered but still Irish! As I have realised since, the baptism in the Holy Spirit will grant you power, but does not remove the need for character development and the discipleship process of making wise decisions.

Later in the book, I will share with you some of the traumatic strug-

YOU DID What?!

gles I went through in that period. Right now, though, I want to highlight the wonderful raw faith and zeal we can enjoy before we get all religious and educated about our Christian life. I knew nothing! But I knew I was empowered.

Then one day, I heard a preacher make a statement that was to revolutionise my life. My initial responses to it, as you are about to read, were extreme and must have tried God's grace to the max. Yet He honoured them long enough for me to discover vitally needed balance. I am not suggesting that anyone reading this should go out and imitate my story, as each one's story is as God uniquely crafts it and/or allows it.

Okay ... here we go.

I have hesitated about putting this bit in the book due to the strong possibility that many of you will think it is simply made up! However unbelievable it may appear, it most certainly is true.

I was working for a very large stock company in Auckland as an assistant to the insurance clerk. I was at the bottom of the food chain.

Suddenly everything changes! I get redeemed, filled with the Holy Spirit and convinced that I am invincible. Then came the day when I heard that phrase from the preacher: *I can do all things through Christ who empowers me* [see Philippians 4:13].

All things! It hit me like a thunderbolt - I could do absolutely anything! I knew nothing of the biblical qualifications, the character teachings I later learnt, the proper and appropriate ways of interpreting Scripture, seeking God for His will first of all, etc. etc. I knew of nothing else but that I could now do **ALL** things!

Looking back, I shudder at my lack of wisdom, grace and biblical balance; but I also recognise that the raw unqualified nature of my trust in God's miraculous was in fact God-given. Tragically, sometimes in our attempts to gain balance, we so often lose that unqualified faith and have to rediscover it later in life. Such has been my own journey.

Let's face it. I was 20 years of age, Irish and now capable of 'all things', being an assistant to the insurance clerk was not an exciting long-term vocation in life. I decided to pursue significance. To be honest, it was not just raw human ambition, but a genuinely held conviction that if I served a supernaturally-empowering God, my life should have a truly supernatural potential. I reasoned that a normal average mortal could do this job, and went to see the manager about stepping up the ladder. I boldly marched in and asked him for an increase of salary from $37 a week to $40 a week.

His response hit me with the force of an ego-shattering sledge hammer: "McCracken, you are not worth $40 a week!" I was utterly stunned. Did he not know that I could now do 'all things'? Did he not understand the enormity of my supernatural potential? What was the matter with this man? I squared off and declared, "Sir, I resign! Mark your calendar and two years from this day, I will walk back through this door and I will be earning more than you!"

Well, I was now unemployed. But what did that matter when one was capable of doing 'all things'?

I went home and looked through the newspaper for a job which would need skills far and above my natural ability. Advert after advert, page after page, and suddenly, there it was - "Legal Executive Wanted for Major Law Firm". Outstanding! Now that would take a miracle! In fact for one who had never been to university and had never read a single law book, it would take a miracle as large as the parting of the Red Sea! That job was mine.

Now, in order for truth to prevail here, the fancy title was more describing of what and who they would train you to become. However,

YOU DID What?!

it still demanded a major miracle for me to get the job.

When I arrived for the interview in my somewhat overly casual attire, I was awed at the surroundings and the important people in their expensive suits. A very dignified middle-aged lady with an air of authority asked me to follow her and I was ushered in to this enormous office of one of the partners. He asked me to be seated and then proceeded to interview me for the position.

After noting the lack of anything impressive in my resume and, no doubt, wondering how I got an interview, he began to ask about my capabilities to do the job and began to list the things that would be required of someone in that position of considerable responsibility. All that filled my mind was, "I can do all things!" The questions were irrelevant as 'all things' was, quite obviously, an unqualified promise of me being able to supernaturally accomplish whatever tasks he gave me regardless of my complete human inability to understand them, let alone achieve them. So, my standard reply was an absolute yes regardless of the task under discussion.

He was amazed. He said he had never anticipated having an interview with someone who could do the entire list! I was hired and went home jubilant.

As I arrived on the following Monday to start work, the same very dignified middle-aged lady with an air of authority asked me to follow her and I was ushered in to another awesome, mahogany-lined office with a huge desk and a magnificent leather chair. It was on the 11th floor and overlooked the Auckland domain. I asked the very dignified middle-aged lady with an air of authority whose office this was. Her answer was, "Mr McCracken, this is your office." About then, reality began to dawn.

While still reeling under this introduction to reality, the partner who hired me entered the room. He had with him a very large pile of manila folders which he placed upon my desk. He left and returned with another pile of manila folders. He left and returned yet again with another pile of manila folders. This reality thing was starting to settle in big time!

He informed me that these were the files of people who had not paid their rates for one of the local councils, and that for years, the firm had been given the responsibility to recover them. He went on to say that their recovery rate had been dismal and it was now my turn to bring the full weight of the law to bear and improve that rate of recovery. That reality thing was now a large, grotesque monster laughing its head off at me!

He left the room and left me to my task. I stared at those folders. That's it. I just stared at them. That reality thing was now screaming that I should run out of the office and not stop until I was under the sheets in my bedroom!

But there was another voice, and it was the voice which had led me to that room from the very beginning. It simply said, "I can do all things." Great! But how? It was then I heard that voice complete the sentence, "...through Christ who empowers me." They say a drowning man surrounded by sharks is unlikely to use a lot of 'thee' and 'thou' words and that he seldom gets into long theological prayers. His prayer is more likely to be, "Heeelp!!!" So that is what I prayed!

Without understanding any of the theology, I was experiencing the first of many hundreds of occasions to come, in which I became acutely aware of my desperate need for the Holy Spirit to talk to me and instruct me in that which I had never learned humanly. And He is so faithful. As I listened, I heard Him say, *"They are all just people. Talk to them and I will give you favour."* That was it. No need to look up one of the many available leather bound volumes, no need to think of magistrates and courts, just 'talk to them'. And that is exactly what I did. One by one, I picked a file, I prayed for the Holy Spirit to help me, and I 'talked to them'. The success rate was staggering.

Approximately 12 months later, with the recovery rate now soaring into previously unknown stratospheres and the firm thinking I was Perry Mason, it hit me one morning - "The honeymoon is over. Any time about now they are going to ask you to do something else and they will discover you know exactly zero about law!" Besides, although I was on a great salary, it was not quite enough to fulfil my prophecy to my previous boss. So, I handed in my resignation, gained a most generous testimonial to my amazing achievements, and went back to searching the newspaper.

This time it was "Office Manager and Company Accountant". Fantastic. My father had been an accountant and had made sure it was one of my subjects at school. I actually knew which side of the balance sheet the assets were!

It was a large importing firm and, of course, a thousand miles beyond my total lack of human qualifications for the job. However, upon reading of my brilliance as a legal executive and hearing my own confession of being able to do anything, the owner decided to throw sanity and logic aside and give me a 3 month trial. The minute I faltered, the job was over. I was once again swimming in a shark-infested sea without a life jacket. Time for another "Heeelp!!!" Once again, it was a year or so of God's unbelievable mercy, grace and enabling as the Holy Spirit spoke His instructions to me day after day.

Why He chose to help me in my rash presumption I really don't know; other than He saw that I really was so very passionate about loving Him, and fierce in my belief that absolutely nothing was too hard for Him. Somewhere in that process, I established that it really was not me who could do anything, but Him. I was fully dependent upon Him and daily confessed that. My total lack of education and training for these positions meant nothing to a Creator who knew everything and was willing to share His knowledge with a desperate young man who cried out to Him for it.

After some months of daily miracles and the unbelievable taking place, my new boss gave me a raise. I knew the moment had arrived. With whatever small amount of humility I could scrape up, I went to see my former boss and showed him my pay slip. It really was one of the sweetest days I had ever experienced! "McCracken, you are not worth $40 a week!" had finally been answered by that which only a supernatural God (and One with infinite grace and long-suffering) could have accomplished. I smiled, shook his hand and we actually became friends of some sort.

As I walked out of his office that day, I could sense another challenge was on its way. My 'office manager' days were about to end.

YOU DID What?!

Chapter Seven

ICE CREAM TO ESKIMOS

What an exciting two years it had been.

Initially, my 'faith' had simply been tolerated by the God of mercy who, knowing my love for Him, decided by His sheer grace to back up my lunacy. I think He does that more times than we know. But during that time, I began to discover that although He may choose to honour such times of bold ignorance, He is far more interested in our listening and in our obedience.

I must stress here that my journey (like your own) is a unique one. We should never seek to imitate another's story. It would be true to say that many Christians today who are successful in their secular vocation, are that way because they have diligently applied themselves to one company for many years and proven faithful there. In fact, that would be the majority. God has honoured their diligence and commitment.

However, the principles of the Kingdom are constant and apply to us all. He simply orders our individual journey and applies those principles so that they are given maximum potential to mould our lives in order to fulfil our future calling and destiny.

Approximately 12 months after I joined the importing firm, I got that restless feeling once again and began to pray and ask Father what it was He wanted me to do. I got the most overwhelming feeling that He wanted me to start my own business. However, I knew nothing of running a business nor did I know anything about any particular field that would lend itself to such an endeavour. As I continued to pray, He reminded me of a time when I had worked for an office equipment and furnishing company for a few months, and the idea of "Zadok Office Furnishings" was born. (Zadok was the name of a priest in the Old Testament and I thought it might increase God's alertness if I used a biblical name!)

I resigned from the importing firm and made myself available for whatever God had in mind for me to do to start this new company. It was 'jump off the deep end' time again. But now it was even more so due to another most wonderful event that had just taken place in my life - marriage!

I will tell you more about that in the next chapter, but sufficient to say that my responsibilities financially had increased. This now demanded of me a whole new level of faith when considering leaving a very well paid job to go out on a limb based on a simple word from the Lord. When I look back now I am in awe of how skilfully and meticulously He orders our steps and prepares us for the life He has chosen for us. This insert of raw faith was to be a vital part of who He was forging me to be.

Whilst in prayer one day, the idea popped into my head that I was to get manufacturers' brochures on various office furniture items, and simply walk down the main street of Auckland City to try and sell them. So that is what I did.

When I sold my first desk, I rang up the manufacturer and informed him. He wanted to know where my showroom was and I replied that I didn't have one. He wanted to know how long I had been in business and I told him that it was the first day. He wanted to know how big the company was and I declared to him that I was it. He then asked if I was nuts! I then further informed him that I had sold his desk and that he shouldn't be worried about silly little details when I could increase his business significantly if he would let me. And that was the way it went on day two, and on day three, and on day four.

I eventually took on two business partners who financed an office and staff, and things began to grow.

One day, I was in my office praying as to what I should do next as we had gone well but really needed a major breakthrough. Father spoke to me to go along to a very large national finance company which had offices in most cities in this nation and was a huge corporation in New Zealand at that time. I grabbed my briefcase and headed off. As I got to the main foyer, I saw the sign "Purchasing Division" and headed to the appropriate floor. As I got there, I noticed that the receptionist was not there and so I continued on and followed the signs to "Group Purchasing Manager".

When I found his office, his secretary wasn't there either, so I simply knocked on his door. Supposing me to be his secretary, he called for me to enter, which I did. He looked up and wanted to know who I was and how I got into his office. I informed him that he had invited me to enter a few seconds before. He ordered me out of his office. I asked for a few moments of his time and said that he had nothing to lose and everything to gain as I was his best news all year.

He turned out to be a certain backslidden Baptist and we talked for over an hour on God's love. Then I remembered why I was there. After having commented about my audacity and that I could 'sell ice cream to Eskimos in the middle of winter', he agreed to give me one test run to furnish an office they were opening up downstairs. Something I had no training in and really knew nothing about. In addition to which, I was partially colour-blind! So I prayed and asked the Holy Spirit to teach me yet again. The result was that within a few months, we had the contract for the entire corporation.

Friends, of this I am certain - my Father can do more with one twinkle of His eyeball than all our human striving can produce in a million years! If only we could learn to depend upon Him and, in simplicity and abandonment, do exactly what He tells us to do.

On another occasion, it was announced that IBM in Melbourne, Australia, was launching a new 'Rebuilt IBM' programme for their typewriters (before the days of computers!). Furthermore, they would be looking for companies in New Zealand to tender for the rights to sell them there. This was a process that took used IBM typewriters and updated them by restoring the non-moving parts and replacing the movable parts. They could then supply them as 'rebuilts' at a much reduced cost to that of a new IBM typewriter. Competition for the contract was expected to be huge as all saw it as a most lucrative potential for any sales company. The mark-up margins for the retailer were close to 80%, and the major players would be pulling out all stops to win the prize.

Once again, the Holy Spirit whispered in my ear the intent of Father. He said I was to get on a plane and fly unannounced to Melbourne, walk into the IBM headquarters there and claim the contract. So that was what I did. It wasn't logical. It wasn't reasonable. It wasn't even intelligent. It had a touch of crazy in there somewhere but obedience can often look a little like that.

At IBM, I reasoned that they had everything to gain and nothing to lose. If I was a failure, they could go ahead with their original plan. If I was successful, they would have saved themselves a very costly launch in Auckland. The outcome was that they also exercised a considerable amount of 'faith'. I think they were just stunned at my raw audacity. Against all logic and sane reasoning, they put aside all the major players and agreed to give me a trial period of 3 months. Well, 3 months was all it took for the Lord to do well beyond all their expectations and the contract was ours from that time on.

I wonder how many anxiety-ridden nights and committee-filled days I would have been subject to if I had sought to reason with the simplicity of that small quiet voice saying, *"Get on a plane to Melbourne."* One of the statements which I believe is the secret to living a successful, overcoming Christian life is "Hear and Obey". It really is that simple, yet so many spend their entire Christian lives seeking ways and methods to substitute that truth with something infinitely more complicated. Why? Because they seek to maintain an element of human involvement and control that the simplicity of 'hear and obey' denies them. It's really kind of sad.

YOU DID *What?!*

Chapter Eight

I DISCOVER ADAM'S RIB

Margaret was my very first girlfriend and we had dated since we were 5 years old. We at no time even looked at another of the opposite sex and spoke throughout our high school years together of the wonderful God-given destiny He had for us as future man and wife. Ours was a courtship of decades, a fairy-tale of childhood romance, of single-minded devotion, of having eyes only for each other from the earliest of years. Even when our friends started teenage dating, we reserved our times together for church picnics and attending prayer meetings.

All of which, of course, is a complete fairy tale!!

YOU DID What?!

Margaret and I did not meet each other until we were twenty one and even then, only from a distance due to my being engaged to another young lady at the time. We were in the same youth group in the same church. That was it.

Then two significant things took place.

The first one was that my then fiancé and I agreed that, although great friends, it was not the will of God for us to get married.

As this was the second time I had been engaged with a similar result, it left me devastated and I concluded that the last thing I wanted to think about for a few hundred years was another romantic relationship.

The second thing was that just prior to the above event, YWAM had come to our area and the local youth were asked to be involved in 'Community Evangelism' going door to door. The leadership decided it was only fair to team up a more experienced person with a person who had not done it before. I was teamed up with Margaret and was expected to take the lead and 'show her the ropes'. The time itself went really well and I thought that was all there was to it.

After my broken engagement, I went through a period of splendid isolation from any potential romantic involvement. I was flatting with two close friends and together we were determined to serve the Lord no matter the cost.

However, my awareness of Margaret and her obvious love for God was increasing and I felt myself being drawn to her more and more. Then one amazing night, we agreed that I would drive her home so we could sit in the car in the driveway of her parents' home and pray for two of our friends who were breaking off their relationship. All I can tell you is that as she started to pray, it hit me like a thunderbolt of clarity - I was going to marry this girl!

Over the next few months, we started to go out to the odd function together and it was obvious that we were falling in love. My friends saw this and were deeply concerned. To prove their own single-mindedness for God's Kingdom, they had both just broken off with their respective girlfriends and now urged me to do the same. After a major time of being inspired by them to pay the ultimate cost, I went forth to make that decision.

Well, I did make it. I proposed!

Three months later we were married and, at the time of this writing, have been married for over 42 years. The wedding was the first our pastor had ever done and we were his guinea pigs! He actually forgot to tell me that I could "now kiss the bride" and so I urgently whispered to him that it was the appropriate moment. He promptly announced my eagerness to the entire congregation!

After the wedding, we went back to Margaret's place to get changed and be farewelled off on our honeymoon. Our faith journey had just commenced.

Neither of us had much money and the only car we had was an old Anglia that Margaret owned. However, in those days, love really was enough if you knew it was God who had put you together. Although I was earning a good salary, I hadn't saved a cent due to an imbalanced view of 'giving it all to Jesus'. Margaret was in a similar position but had been more diligent and managed to buy that little Anglia car. However, that purchase had consumed most of whatever she had. We had very little money and I was about to take my new bride off to a week's honeymoon in the Bay of Islands and return to a flat without the rent money, let alone anything for food. Margaret was learning that our life was not really going to be at all 'normal'.

As we embraced parents, shook hands, and became the subject of many well-meaning jokes, we moved towards the car. The wedding

YOU DID *What?!*

Daily Provision

had been great, our relatives and friends were the best, but we knew if we could but only reach that car, we could escape! It was then that our Great Provider began to show us what our life journey was going to be like. With the shaking of the hand came the urging to take 'a little something', as various ones felt to give to us spontaneously. Later, when we took the money out of my pocket and counted it, there was enough to cover the honeymoon, the first week's rent and our first purchase of groceries. And that was how we started our married life.

Daily Prayed God would Supply

We lived in a small flat under a house. It was old, tiny and slightly decaying. As strange as it would sound to most young couples today, we actually loved it! We were together. We daily prayed for God's supply and enthusiastically gave whatever wasn't necessary for immediate needs to the local church and missionary endeavours. Even when the money came rolling in from my business, we felt compelled by the Lord to sow that finance into the vision that our pastor had for the building of a Christian campsite at Snell's Beach, north of Auckland. Saving up for a house or future trips away did not seem to be an option worthy of much discussion.

To me, it is a pity that today so many insist on so much before they venture on their journey together. Parents seem to be willing to sacrifice even their own retirement funds to ensure that the next generation never have to face the challenges which, in fact, were so fundamental in making their own generation so strong. The values forged in hardships, of learning to depend upon each other, and of trusting God for the basics are largely avoided.

Consequently, I believe that in this generation, many married couples (not all, of course) have a severe lack in the areas of appreciation, gratitude, believing God and anticipation of His supply. They have been robbed of what made this nation strong - the pioneering spirit. Such times were invaluable in preparing us both for what was to lie ahead.

Develop a pioneering Spirit

So began our years of married life. Years of being stretched, challenged, adjusted, changed, shaken, broken, convicted; and worked upon constantly by the Divine Surgeon, who seemed to never run out of creative ways to use Margaret and myself as His primary scalpel on each other. Marriage has a lot to do with God having His way in the gaining of the life-transformations that He intends to bring to pass in us all. Oh, how true the immortal declaration: "Love is blind but marriage is a big eye-opener!"

When people hear us share on the subject of marriage today and see the strength that God has given to our relationship, they know so little of those difficult years. Years in which our marriage was hard, demanding and often filled with despair. Questions and tears drove us many times to complete discouragement. We have often said there were times when the only thing that kept us together was our love for God, and the firmly-held conviction that divorce was not an option.

They were also wonderful years of discovery, learning, being inspired as we saw answers together, being prepared to apply biblical principles and rejoicing over God's interventions of grace. I so thank the Lord that Margaret was (and is) one who would not quit when the going was tough, that she knew how to cast herself on God and persevere. She also had (and still does) this passion for excellence in marriage and family life. We certainly have not attained to full excellence (or anything like it), but the measure of it that we now enjoy is most certainly due to our unswerving commitment to that goal.

And throughout those years, God has written a message in our hearts which He now uses (and has for four decades) in bringing recovery and instruction to thousands of marriages, especially those of leaders. Without the trauma and the heartache, there would have been no reason for our crying out to Him for answers. And without the discovery of those answers, there would not have been the life-saving seminars and resources that God has graced us with for the sake of others.

YOU DID *What?!*

I have learnt that all of life is God's instrument to prepare us for His ultimate purpose. I have learnt that *all things work together for good to those who love God* [see Romans 8:28]. I have learnt that the pursuit of excellence and managing the realities of pain are not exclusive of each other; they are allies. I have learnt that you can be super-spiritual as Elijah, but if you do not possess a committed resolve to please Father and stay the course regardless, you will probably quit and walk away like so many have done.

I have learnt that one must enter marriage with a 'divorce is not an option' conviction which becomes the anchor when that option screams out in its enticement. I have learnt that praying together is not only essential in our relational healing but, when prayed from pure and passionate hearts, has the power to deny the enemy his objectives and turn the event from tragedy to triumph. I have learnt that in the pursuit of our becoming the expressions of Christ that He wants us to be, the most painful chapters are the most vital and the most valuable. I have learnt to trust my Father in such times and I have learnt that He is utterly worthy of that trust.

During my years with Margaret, there have also been days of wonder - days of romance and affection, days of sunsets and roses, days of strolling on beaches, and communicating love and desire. There have also been days of sharing and caring, days of tender comfort and constant support, and days of being the pillar in each other's lives.

These years have also seen us standing shoulder to shoulder in the heat of the battle, of holding on to each other in the dark nights of the soul, of confronting the adversary by the power of agreement, of storming the next bunker knowing that we can depend on one another. There have been days of faith and adventure, of scary dependence and learning to trust, of excitement over never knowing where the next dollar was coming from as God so wonderfully supplied, of walking on water, and of boldly marching into the mist of the unknown.

I discovered that this awesome woman by my side is made of steel in areas of resolve, yet so very compassionate and sensitive to the pain of others. She has a stubborn tenacity when a job needs doing, yet so responsive when listening to the opinion of another. There isn't a demon in hell that does not fear her lioness' instincts when it comes to protecting her children, and her ruthlessness in pruning roses has you silently thanking God that she is on your side.

Margaret has walked beside me through life; through storms and testings, tempests and trials, sacrifices and faith. She has never flinched nor been guilty of unbelief. She has dared to live out of her comfort zone married to a redeemed Irish lunatic, who God asks to do the impossible. She has experienced months of not knowing where the next meal would come from, or how the mortgage would be paid. She has pioneered, and she has dealt with grief and pain. She has stared despair in the face and conquered. She has wept until tears were inadequate yet never became bitter. She has forgiven me and embraced me when I have failed, and rejoiced with me in times of breakthrough. She fills my heart with awe and my mouth with gratitude that God would give such a one to me.

Margaret is my inspiration, my God-given goad to excellence, my reminder that exaggeration is lying, my Christlike example, my love partner, and the most amazingly selfless mother and grandmother I have ever seen. For the most bewildering of reasons, she is my best fan, my cheerleader, my encourager, and the one who tells me that it can be done.

Margaret is, and always will be, my best friend. It doesn't get much better than that!

YOU DID *What?!*

Chapter Nine

FIRE AND RHETORIC

It is at this point that I must fill in some gaps.

When I returned from Fiji with YWAM, I discovered within me a burning desire to serve the Lord full-time. In those days, that meant either becoming an evangelist, or pastoring a local church or being on staff with one. The latter was not likely as this was prior to anything even resembling a large church, let alone a mega church. A large church in those days was anything over 100 people and that included counting babies still in the womb!

With my only experience of Christian service then was being on the

YOU DID What?!

streets with Teen Challenge or on the mission field with YWAM, I knew I was called to win souls to Christ by whatever means opened up to me. However, I also had a yearning to know more about this Christian life and the Bible, which drove me to investigate the options of Bible Schools. Attending a full-time one was out of the question as I would have gone nuts being cloistered away with books and learning, and being off the streets of frontline evangelism. So I looked for what was available in part-time studies.

I was then still a member of a non-Charismatic local church, back in the days before the Charismatic Renewal. I had become a real concern with my 'Pentecostal' experiences and my escapades in Fiji with what they considered a fringe para-church organisation. My pastor saw my claim to the baptism of the Holy Spirit as being most alarming.

My Dad and Mum were members of the Methodist church, and up until my original born again experience at age 16, so was I. In fact, my middle name "Wesley" was given due to Dad's heritage with the Wesleyan Methodists in Northern Ireland. Even though Dad had lost almost all of his original ministry zeal for the Lord and had become a restless soul (we lost count of the number of house shifts as children), he retained a deep reverence towards the Lord and knew the way of salvation. I shared with him my hunger and my recent experiences and his response was amazing. He said that Wesley had also had such an experience with the Holy Spirit and had called it "The Second Blessing". He seemed genuinely moved that I had received it.

When I shared my quest for a part-time Bible School with him, he did not hesitate. He reminded me of a tent evangelist he had taken us as a family to hear several times. It was part of Dad's own quest to find peace for himself and salvation for us as a family. The evangelist's name was Rob Wheeler, and he had recently closed the tent down and leased a large building in Auckland (Haddon Hall) in which to open up a local church. This is where Dad recommended for me to go. One of the most vital steps of my life was, once again, due to my Dad's sincere desire to see me follow the calling that was on my life to serve the Lord. I am so very grateful that even in the midst of his own challenges, his honouring of God and his love for his boys made him available to the Holy Spirit on such occasions.

The church, which had been kind to me in Hamilton in the Teen Challenge and YWAM days, belonged to a group called "The Indigenous Churches of New Zealand". Today they are known as "The New Life Churches of New Zealand". I discovered that Pastor Rob Wheeler was a member of that same group and was considered to be an apostle among them. This was confirmation to me of Dad's advice and I applied to go to the evening Bible College run by Auckland Christian Fellowship. The year was 1966 and I was 19 years of age. This family of churches was to become my own spiritual family for the following 26 years, and I still have a good relationship with them today. Good friends are like that; they stand the test of time.

I arrived in Auckland so very glad that this church was going to have the honour of my presence. I was saved, water baptised, filled with the Holy Spirit, and evangelising anything that twitched! But it could not be said that I had yet discovered humility!

My 3 years with Rob were ones of learning the Bible from an amazing teacher of the Word, and being released by him to evangelise on the streets of Auckland. We would preach on the street corners and also in the tent, which we would put up in various vacant lots and places allowed by the Council. Many a night I would take my turn preaching with great fire and rhetoric to huge crowds of 7-9 people, many of whom would walk out before I finished.

We never did see our dream of putting the 'Billy Graham Crusades' into second place become a reality, but it was a great opportunity to develop one's preaching skills and endurance potential. By the sheer mercy of God for broken people, we did have the joy of leading a few to Christ. There definitely were fruit from those days, but I must confess that many of our descriptions of the meetings to others at that time would have made a fisherman's tale seem conservative. We had a lot of "the one that got away" stories!

Rob was the <u>ultimate encourager</u>. He never ceased to inspire us and release us. His faith and personal passion was contagious, and his knowledge of the Word was a great foundation for my future years of ministry. His encouragement knew no bounds, as in the case of my singing. It would not be true to say that I have never been a singer, but only that I could never sing in tune. In fact, the sounds I would make when attempting to do so would have a similar effect as when one listens to the scraping of fingernails down a blackboard. Nerves get frayed when I sing. Rob's answer to this dilemma was to put me in the choir and appoint me as one of the chief worship leaders for Sunday night meetings! No one could dispute the enormity of that man's faith!

Encouraged, taught, inspired, understanding end-time events, tent-trained, and top marks in the Bible School. I was ready for the Church! But was the Church ready for me?

The one thing that had not been addressed was my character and in particular, my monumentally-sized ego. That was when God transferred me to the 'Marines'.

Chapter Ten

JOINING THE 'MARINES'

We have a term today in parenting: 'tough love'. Well, God is more than capable of that when He sees that the size of your ego has far outstripped the disciplines of servanthood and humility.

I had not yet found a will stronger than my own, and my appearance of godliness was only because no one really crossed that will or challenged my sovereignty over it. That was when God decided that a tap on the shoulder wouldn't do it. He called a summit meeting of the Trinity and it was decided that the gloves would have to come off if tough love was the only way of ensuring my pride would be sufficiently blown to smithereens. They decided to send me to boot camp. They looked for a 'drill instructor' who would love me, teach me, correct me, discipline me, toughen me for the frontline, and kick my butt when it was necessary! They introduced me to Shaun Kearney.

Life in the fast lane was about to change.

Shaun was over 6 feet tall with eyeballs which, with just one glance, could melt steel bars at a hundred paces. Demons would tremble, deacons would melt, and giant-sized egos would cringe. He taught with revelation, preached with fire and prophesied like 'Elijah' on a good day. He was undoubtedly one of the most powerful prophets in New Zealand at that time and a considerable force to be reckoned with. He pioneered the breaking down of barriers between different Pentecostal streams. He was the driving force which resulted, eventually, in the initial historic gatherings of the Associated Pentecostal Churches of New Zealand.

I had met my match.

My first few months in the church where Shaun was the pastor were filled with violently mixed emotions. On the one hand, I was impacted so powerfully by his preaching, his standards of no compromise (sadly lacking in so many places today) and his amazing prophetic gift. Yet on the other, I was bewildered by his apparent oblivion to my own gigantic hugeness of spirituality. Did this man not know the greatness which had been placed in his midst?

Well, yes. He understood all too clearly and he also knew that before dealing with that ego, he had to starve it a little. He knew that to give me recognition too early and to further boost my pride by neglecting discipleship, would be to ultimately see me destroyed by it. It is sad that so very little discipleship or addressing of character issues is done by senior leaders today in their training of the next generation.

Audacious Faith Adventures in the Life of David McCracken

Giftedness and achievement should never be allowed to be built beyond the strength of character foundations. To ignore this principle is to invite disaster in the later life of that young ministry.

My time with Shaun eventually saw me develop in the prophetic gift and the seeds of my later ministry as a prophet were sown into my heart at that time. Under his leadership I learnt about faith, the presence of the Holy Spirit, tithing, authority and submission, celebration, and the vital nature of the local church in God's plan for saving the world in the end times. Shaun believed in the glorious Church, the triumphant Church, and the Bride of Christ in purity and power. He taught us about Church Government and how the pastor, supported by an eldership, was responsible for the well-being of God's people when they voluntarily chose to submit to that oversight.

In time, Shaun began to use me more and more. But God knew that ego of mine needed a lot of work yet and so He orchestrated conditions to press my button and reveal it for what it was. He does the same for us all, but so often we end up rebuking the devil or our leader rather than thanking God for His loving perseverance.

One such incident happened when we were sent as a young people's group to Whangarei, a town some 3 hours north of Auckland. We were to sing and testify in their Sunday service. I was not a leader at that time but simply one in the group.

Due to my eventual calling as a prophet, I had a fierce sense of black and white righteousness. Compromise and 'worldliness' was like a red flag to a bull and I often mistook my Irish-driven passion and Pharisaic religious fervour for true spirituality. As we assembled to sing, I noticed that a young lady in our group was wearing a mini-skirt (well, above the knees anyhow) and she was in the front row! Oh, the shame of it! Could she not see the damage to the 'cause' of Christ?! I swiftly came to her side and in a fire-breathed whisper that would have terrorised 'Braveheart', I hissed, "Get to the back of the group, you hussy. How dare you wear that on such an occasion!!" Then with God's honour suitably defended and one less-worthy mortal sent to weep in the shadows, I returned to sing 'Amazing grace, how sweet the sound'!

We returned to Auckland and in the evening two days later (still in my singlehood days), I was relaxing in the flat I shared with my two best friends, who were also Shaun's disciples. These two had often shared that there was no force of nature nor demon from hell that would make them desert me in a time of need; their loyalty and courage would stand any test this world could bring. We were the 3 musketeers of the Kingdom; inseparable in famine and war; shoulder to shoulder in battle; facing all odds without flinching; side by side, noble and true. But then one of them looked out the window. His face went white as he stared down the driveway. He whirled around to my other friend and declared, "There is only one man alive who can make Shaun that mad!", and they both looked at me. As Shaun came in (or was it through?) the front door, my two valiant armour-bearers went out the back door! They barely had time to yell, "Hi, Shaun! Bye, Shaun!"

Shaun was at his magnificent best; blazing, fire-balling, 'Mt. Sinai' stuff that would have had me in awe if I was not the subject of it. At least the Israelites had rocks to hide under, but for me there was nothing. "Sit!!" I sat. His finger was now fully extended and mere inches from the tip of my nose. My blood pressure must have reached 200 as sweat burst out on my brow and upper lip, and the palms of my hands dripped. "There is only one pastor in this church, and it isn't you!!"

What followed was revelation upon revelation. Incredible insights into the filthy ugliness of my pride and the lawlessness of my unrestrained ego; I had confused a zeal for righteousness with monumental arrogance and an insensitive, non-caring abuse that was inexcusable; people like me had to be broken or end up destroying themselves and everyone else around them; I was a rebellious, self-willed egomaniac who, unrestrained, would wreak havoc upon the church. I had no idea of the repercussions of that one small, spontaneous, whispered comment to a girl in a mini-skirt!

The thing I remember about Shaun is that you never had to learn the same lesson twice. Really, truly, honestly! Once really was enough.

And every time I hear of yet another unbroken, self-willed, bright young potential ministry star that self-destructs because of the lack of ever having had the privilege of boot camp, I pause to say a heartfelt "Thanks!" If you are reading this Shaun, I remain to this day indescribably grateful for that particular season in my life, and that Father orchestrated you to be such a significant part of it.

Am I suggesting that we all should train others that way? Of course not. It was a different era, a different season. I have no doubt that I was an exceptional case which required an exceptional 'Elijah', and Shaun and I would both agree that not all things were done perfectly. What I am saying is we must have more involved and committed 'fathers in the faith', who not only love us with a tenderness and with humility, but care enough to tell us the truth. We need those who will work on our character flaws so that yet another generation does not fall into the ditch while others look on and all-knowingly declare, "I could see that coming, you know." If Shaun 'saw it coming', he did something about it.

I need to stress here that there were also times of sincere fatherly affection. I never doubted Shaun's love and he demonstrated it so many times when he knew we needed Father's love in human form. Challenges in our marriage, challenges with our children, and my own internal struggles with humanity, were met with a father's care and wise counsel.

In my early prophetic moments when I would hesitate with the importance of a word that God had given me, he was there to encourage and support me. One time, I received a word of a very challenging nature for a very well-known international ministry. Shaun questioned me until convinced and then took me to see that ministry and stated his confidence in me. He dared to put his own reputation on the line because he believed in me. Loyalty was a two-way street with Shaun. We need those who will love enough to confront, but confront with care. What I call 'carefrontation'.

We need drill sergeants, we need a good dose of the 'Marines', and we need a new generation who isn't intimidated with the first smell of battle nor offended when their leader tells them to "Sit!" We need to turn the sheepfolds into army barracks and transform pew-warming, entertainment-seeking, mellow-puffs into conquest-minded overcomers. We need a generation who is not in it for the furtherance of their own ego, image or reputation, but to better serve a blood-stained Saviour whose sacrifice and love demands their devotion.

Forgive my bluntness, but thinking of my beloved prophet (as he was then), reminds me that we are not born to sit under pomegranate trees having a picnic, but born for the front line [see story in 1 Samuel 14].

As such lessons began to penetrate, Margaret and I were sent by Shaun to play a significant role in ministering to Methodists and Congregationalists in farming areas north of Auckland. This we did midweek in the evenings after work, often not arriving back until midnight or later, and having to face another full day of business or employment in the morning. Tiredness took second place to the joy of ministering and seeing ones come to Christ, be baptised in water and then filled with the Holy Spirit.

I will never forget one of those baptisms. There was a river estuary in Maungaturoto, which was a great spot for such events. The water was about the right depth while the bank allowed for cars to park with their lights on so that we could see. It also meant that spectators could, and they often did, gather for the occasion.

There was just one small snag. In winter, the water temperature accompanied by a chilling wind factor was enough to give you hypothermia! On this particularly cold night, we considered calling it off but our desire to see folks baptised overcame our hesitation. By the time we had baptised 3 or 4, the spectators were beginning to think that the Holy Spirit must have been most heavy in His anointing upon us. We had all started to change colour and shake violently. Apparently they had heard of such things in the early days of Pentecost. By the time number 6 was done, the blue colour had intensified and the chattering of teeth could be heard in Wellington! We didn't want to disillusion them, but at some stage we had to tell them that we were not so much anointed, as we were frozen!

Those weekly trips to north of Auckland gave me moments of instruction that were to last a lifetime. Today when instructing churches and pastors in the proper use of the prophetic gift, I often refer to those moments of instruction. I will share one with you.

The farmers had gathered and the singing was under way as we arrived after the considerably long trip. Tired from a full day of work and battling traffic out of the city, we had met together on the North Shore and piled into one car to drive for approximately two hours to get there. We were tired but, as always, excited about what God would do in our time together.

As the meeting got under way, the worship and spontaneous praise filled the room with the presence of God and I felt the urge to prophesy over some of those gathering. With each prophecy, my boldness grew and my remembrance of instruction dimmed. It was so exciting! Cautions are often forgotten when you get excited. This was the case as I came upon one of the young farmers who belonged to the local Congregationalist church. With great authority (accompanied by loads of volume, fervency and sweat), I declared that he would become a recognised, ascension gift, Ephesians 4, teacher to the Body of Christ! Magnificent stuff! We drove home triumphant at yet another night of conquest, and eagerly anticipated our return the following week.

That Sunday morning, Shaun spotted me arriving in the car park and beckoned me over to sit for a moment in the front seat of his car before going into the service. In my dying (but still twitching to be alive) Irish ego, I thought that he had heard about our outstanding meeting and was about to congratulate me in person. What a wonderful moment, to be finally recognised for the true prowess of my gift. I couldn't wait.

Those eyeballs should have been the warning. As the colour changed and the fire began to burn, I nervously began to finger the escape lever on my passenger door. It appeared stuck and I wondered why they had not yet invented ejector seats in cars for such a moment. Then he sucked in air. I was beginning to sweat. And then he started…

"If you ever pull a stunt like that again, you will be grounded for 6 months! Have I taught you nothing? Where do you get off prophesying an ascension gift office over someone without submitting it to Senior Leadership first? Haven't I told you the damage that can cause? What about all prophecy being judged? Was his pastor there? Was I there? Was anybody in real authority there?" He was on an awe-inspiring roll. "To help you remember this for the rest of your life, Googleby (not his real name, but a guy Shaun knew and whom I considered to be a little of a nerd) will take your meeting for the next 5 weeks and you will serve him!" It worked, as I never did it again and I remember it enough to tell you of it right now.

There were many such incidents. You do not forget such moments of instruction easily. Some have suggested that he could have delivered it more delicately and the blazing eyeballs were not necessary. Perhaps for lesser mortals that would be true, but both God and Shaun knew what it would take for that principle to override my pride and lodge in my brain for eternity. It was gladiator stuff, bloodied and scar-filled, but knowing it was the training which would keep you alive made the pain worth it.

One of the major reasons why I have, by God's grace, been accepted as a prophet in so many churches today is that they feel safe with their 'sheep' when I'm around. They tell me they know I will not go in irresponsibly with a blaze of glory and walk out leaving them with 'blood on the floor'. I owe that to boot camp and to a red-haired prophet. I owe it to my Heavenly Father who knew how much tough love was necessary so that I could later run my race with honour.

Today, as bullets fly and controversies rage; as prophets come and go; as men of renown fall from grace; as wild prophetic predictions fail to come to pass; and many church leaders feel that to get a prophet in to speak is like playing Russian roulette with 5 bullets in the chamber; I pause and think of my time in the 'Marines' with a drill sergeant named Shaun, and I am grateful.

What great days they were. Our Christian life was one of total dedication to the 'cause'. Every weekend, 4 or 5 weeknights and most public holidays were filled with services, prayer meetings, working bees, financial sacrifices and outreaches of one sort or another. Christmas holidays were spent each year at 'Christmas Camp' - a time of spiritual sharpening and challenge, inspiration and conviction, revelation and instruction, prayer and celebration, fun with family and friends, and sitting around a blazing fire after the evening meeting laughing and telling stories. Pioneers were being forged and a generation being born who knew what it was to live 100% for the King and His Kingdom. Were we imbalanced? Oh, yes. But has the bulk of the Church in the Western world swung way too far the other way? **OH, YES!**

YOU DID *What?!*

My three years in the 'Marines' with Shaun were the most valuable of my preparation years and I cannot think of them, and Shaun's involvement at that time, without gratitude and affection. It would be true to say that the strength of his leadership was, at times, in need of greater balance in shepherd care and softness of spirit. It would be true to say that not all flourished and some went AWOL rather than submit to the demands made upon them. It would be true to say that some still get angry at the thought of moments when their difference of opinion was stomped on as frivolous rubbish (even though that would have been so in many cases). It would be true to admit that leaders who could wither up resistance with one steely glance would not fit our mould today (and neither should it). It would be true to say that those who did not know him as I knew him, saw him as a mix of Elijah, Paul and Mussolini. But that was because they did not really know him.

He was my spiritual father who genuinely loved me. He was my mentor, my teacher, my prophet, my friend, and the only one who cared enough to kick my butt often enough and hard enough to straighten me out. They say that the drill sergeant is the most resented man in boot camp but the most loved on the battlefield. Why? Because every day a Marine stays alive through exercising a discipline of training, he knows who alone is to be thanked for it. I was in the 'Marines' and Shaun was my drill sergeant. I loved him then and I love him now.

Then came the day when Shaun decided it was time for us to leave the nest. The place picked for our launch into full-time ministry was a suburb in the south of Auckland called Papatoetoe. The church had been there for many years with a number of former pastors, but had now entered a time of decline and very few people remained. There was probably about 30-40, including children. Margaret and I had one toddler and another baby on the way but we were ready for the challenge.

Our season as pioneers was about to begin.

Chapter Eleven

STEPPING ON TO THE WATER

It was February 1973. We were both just 25 years of age and the challenge was huge, but so too was our faith and expectations. In fact, the Sunday before leaving the church in Takapuna, I boldly announced that, "We will have over a hundred by Christmas." I think God must have smiled at that moment.

As I mentioned earlier, during those days of Zadok Office Furnishings, we were blessed and were able to earn a very good income. However, God continually challenged us to give into the work of the Kingdom and consequently we had no nest egg when the 'call' finally came. We were launched and farewelled with the knowledge that love and prayer support would be there, but no financial support. In those pioneer days, it was considered part of the proof of your call that the Lord would miraculously provide for you.

Today churches seem to be planted with much greater understanding and often with considerable personnel and financial guarantee. I do stop and wonder if, in the process, we have lost something of that demand for raw, unqualified faith that the 70s presented. I wonder if the true spirit of the pioneer has, to some degree, become a casualty.

Developing Faith

As I see the constant miracles of provision in our ministry today, I cannot but feel that those early days of crying out to God for the weekly grocery money was God's careful building of the knowledge of His faithfulness into our lives.

Many were the days when we literally did not know where the next dollar would come from. The income of the church was barely enough to cover the rent of the hall and general expenses. They were days of wonder and amazement as we saw the diverse ways the Lord met our needs as a family and as a church. The finance might come from a farmer in the north walking the paddocks, or a Baptist chemist who filled a prescription for me and dreamt about me that night. He may have used a myriad of ways but He was the only Source—our amazingly faithful Father.

Perhaps the most notable in those first few months was the house. When I gave my resignation to my two financial partners at Zadok Office Furnishings (which had continued to grow successfully), I was begged to stay on for just 2-3 days a week. They were willing to pay me a considerable salary which would have been more than enough to live on and the rest of the week would be free for my small congregation. As I prayed about this most generous offer, I felt that the Lord impressed me to decline it because He wanted to be our Supplier. As I look back now I see that it was all part of His unique plan to prepare us for today. Margaret agreed and we declined the offer. We were back to believing God daily for our income.

It was then that God spoke to my former partners (one of them was not a Christian). They rang one day to inform me that it was only honourable that my birthing of the company be recognised financially and that they were going to pay the deposit for us to move into our very own home (our first!). Our own home!

Our first home was the fruit of a principle which has become part of our deepest convictions: when you are willing to die to something out of obedience, God keeps the accounts and can abundantly repay when the time is right. (Not that He has to, as we already owe Him everything and He owes us nothing.)

So there we were, pioneering with 30-40 people.

I organised prayer meetings, mobilised the people to march the streets with door to door evangelism, challenged the people to get on to the frontline, spoke to the local newspaper, advertised, preached and declared that great and mighty things were about to take place. We waited for the multitude to arrive. And we waited.

After some months of preaching to the same group of people, Sunday after Sunday, my frustration was growing and my grace was diminishing. It all came to a head one Sunday night about ten minutes into the preaching of the message. I simply could not take it anymore. I stopped preaching and made a declaration: "Enough! I will not preach one more minute to you bunch! I love you but get out on to the streets and come back with some people!" The early years are often referred to as my 'pre-broken days' and it is obvious to me now that my fiery communications must have been rather challenging at times. With looks that only truly bewildered sheep can express, my congregation filed out to look for the lost in society.

It was about then I realised that I too was one of the sheep. I had to find people! As I drove around the streets of Papatoetoe, I was getting more and more desperate. Desperate people do desperate things. I spotted 4 or 5 people that appeared to be Islanders, waiting at a bus stop. I leapt out of my car and began to powerfully and persuasively invite them to get into my car, which, amazingly, they did. Before they could think too much, I drove like 'Jehu' back to the hall. I ushered them to the front row much to the incredulous stares of the lesser mortals who had returned with no one. Revival had come!

I preached like a man possessed. Rhetoric poured forth and my hands gestured wildly as I savoured my moment of history-making ingathering. Nothing could destroy such a moment. Nothing, that is, other than reality.

About 4 minutes into the message, it dawned on me: they could not understand one word of English! As they stared at me with blank faces creased with beautiful but unknowing smiles, I truly wanted a large hole to open up or the world to suddenly spin off its axis and hurl me into outer space! For some time after that event, whenever I attended the local ministers' gathering, I would be greeted with such comments as: "I hear you're having revival with the Islanders, David!" My humiliation felt like a hundred foot high cross and Jesus' injunction to take it up daily seemed unjust and bewildering.

After another few months of trying everything in the book to draw people and failing, my incredibly 'anointed' preaching had reduced the congregation to just 9 adults. I felt overwhelmed with a sense of personal failure and my mind was daily confronted with the magnificent statement of vision I made to our home church: "We will have over a hundred by Christmas." I finally hit my knees and admitted to God that I could no longer do this. I told Him how desperately I needed Him and that I was willing to do absolutely anything He wanted me to. A friend called Nebuchadnezzar told me that eating grass like an animal can do that to you. He said it brings us to our senses [see Daniel 4:33-34]. It is then that we realise that God builds

His Church and isn't as impressed with our claims to be magnificently gifted as we are. It is then that one remembers that Adam was just a compilation of dust before God breathed life into him.

I think the pain of such moments and the seeing and acknowledging of one's complete insufficiency is infinitely valuable and critical to our spiritual development. However, at the time and to be honest, it stung like rolling around in one's underwear in a bed full of nettles! Isn't it wonderful that at such times, there are always those who will come and inform you that, "Things really are not that bad" or "Hang in there, Jesus loves you" or "Just think of Foxe's Book of Martyrs and it will come into perspective"? I think that such people should be given one way tickets to Pluto.

In my desperate openness, God did finally speak to my heart. He said that I was to close the church in Papatoetoe and pioneer a new one in the next suburb, Manurewa. It really should not have surprised us that much as it was in Manurewa that God had led us to buy our home.

We gathered up our 9 adults plus children and started in Manurewa in the beginning of 1974. Now with two children of our own, a mortgage, hall hire and no income, we continued to daily discover the consistent predictability of God's faithfulness and provision.

We advertised the new beginnings in the local newspaper and from the very first Sunday, we knew something had changed. People started to come and the church began to slowly but definitely grow. Some came because of the small newspaper advertisement while others came because someone said there was a lot of noise coming out of the high school hall on a Sunday morning. We didn't care! They were coming! One lady came because God sovereignly gave her my name when she was putting the washing out on the clothesline. She became our chief intercessor and remains so to this very day. She is our dear and wonderful friend, Jacky Squires (in those days Jacky

Stevens).

We were still pioneers but we could feel the foundations being built.

Chapter Twelve

GIVING GOD GREY HAIRS

Those who have known me for a while refer to my life as the 'pre-broken days' and the 'post-broken days'. We will get to the breaking bit in a later chapter, but right now, I invite you to get a strong cup of coffee, settle in and walk with me through a chapter of those 'pre-broken days'.

In those first few years, there was a saying amongst the ministers in the area: "Crackers (that's what they called me!) does not have many, but wow, are they fanatics!" I really could not understand what they were referring to as I thought it was really all quite normal.

Like the time, inspired by the Salvation Army and without consulting my leadership team, I declared from the pulpit that the entire congregation was going to end up in uniforms and march down the main street, militantly beating huge drums! They forgave me for that one.

Or the time when a man turned up in our church after having escaped from a cult. He informed us that his wife and children were still in there and were brainwashed. His tales of what happened in that place were numbing and tore at your heartstrings. I could feel my Irish indignation growing and a resolve to do something about it was forming in the parts of my brain still given to militant thinking.

We formed our very own commando unit. We rang the local people we knew and asked them for a couple of cars with drivers who were saved enough to be Christians, but not so religious that they had lost their daring and courage. Our team flew down, met the drivers and swooped into the compound. The rest is unprintable but we ended up with the family! The wife went from thinking I was someone to be feared to becoming a great friend, and the children went on to become wonderful Christian young men and women. The majority of those kids today are serving God in various ministry expressions and leadership roles.

Would I recommend that to a youth group today? Not really. It was in an era when such an action would result in public approval, not criminal prosecution and lawsuits as it might do today. Raw? Yes! But wonderfully alive!

Then there were the tales that filtered back to my eldership about how I had acted at the pastors' conferences.

To understand, you have to realise that we did not believe in taking days off back then. We lived a life of zeal and passion that often verged on exhaustion, and then when we got to conferences, we let it all explode on the first night! Other denominations heard about our first night events and wanted to buy tickets!

I remember the very first pastors' conference. I was in awe; they were my heroes of the faith, my mentors, those who had blazed the trail and walked with God. I was so filled with anticipation as we arrived at the campsite in Nelson.

At the close of the first meeting together, we went off to the dormitory. In those pioneer days, there was no staying at the Sheraton or even the local pub. We had a campsite with dorms, one for the ladies and one for the men. It was Spartan but most fitting for those days of conquest-minded pioneers. (I think we have lost something of that in our recent years of 'doing it right'.)

As we men filed into our dorm, we were met with the sight of a huge pile of pyjamas in the middle of the floor. All the tops had been mixed up with different bottoms and then knotted into this endless great rope of entanglement. It was a horrendous mess! As I later found out, my wife was one of the culprits. They had somehow sneaked out while we were having supper and performed this act of treason. (I thought us husbands were supposed to be honoured and respected!)

It was unthinkable that such a thing could go unanswered. We came up with the perfect plan and picked out a select number of those who were considered to be strong and fit, and gave them the commission. They were to go up into the hills out back and return with the enormous black billy goat which was kept there. This they did and then proceeded to the ladies dorm. Opening the door as quietly as one could while trying to wrestle a goliath of its species now steaming in its anger, they launched that beast in to vent its fury on our unsuspecting wives.

Screams rent the air! Shrieks hit high 'C's and we would have almost felt bad about it all if it were not for the fact that we had collapsed in hysterics.

That black billy created havoc! It dropped black balls all over the floor, rampaged from bed to bed, and forced otherwise dignified pastors' wives to stand on their beds experiencing barely redeemable emotions. Then it went for a most dignified lady's dressing gown. With what was now a possessed frenzy, it sank its teeth into the dressing gown and began to eat it! This belonged to the wife of the co-leader of our Movement. We were going to pay for this.

Then, in a blaze of heroism (I can almost hear the 'Superman' theme playing), Margaret launched herself onto that black hulk of devastation and destruction. She wrestled it and (with memories of rodeos in her mind) proceeded to drag it to the door at the far end of the dorm. With wild applause and tears of thanksgiving, her fellow besieged ones expressed their gratitude.

You would have thought that we would be struck with a degree of remorse, but not so. We had fought back and were on a roll. The next thing that happened was such a shock that I almost backslid.

Someone mentioned (it was meant as a joke!) that the ladies were so mad that we should put one of our most esteemed national leaders in there to reason with them. Horrified by the thought, he started to inch towards open space from where he could run. He never made it. Two of our largest legends of the faith pounded after him, caught him, then carrying him somewhat like one would carry a ladder, they kicked open the door and hurled him in!

That sight gave me nightmares. The door would open for a millisecond and we would catch a glimpse of his terrified countenance before it would slam shut again. This happened several times while some of the more strategic-thinking ladies endeavoured to put curlers in his hair. It was getting grim. Something had to be done.

I was standing in a state of disbelief and horror by this stage. These were my heroes of the faith and they were acting barely saved. I was flabbergasted!

As I stood there, one of those very large legends whirled around and grabbed me by the scruff of the neck. He roared at me, "Don't just stand there, boy! Do your duty!" With one decisive stride he hauled me over to where the fire hose was on the wall. As he pushed the nozzle into my hands, he dragged me to the door of the ladies dorm. As he hurled the door open, he shoved me in through the gap with the command to stand my ground at all costs. I took one look at that force of vengeful females and remembered in an instant the wisdom of my father when faced with a similar situation in WW2: "Wisdom is the better part of valour" (loosely translated as 'Run'!!!).

Well, that was my introduction to pastors' conferences. It would be true to say that it wasn't quite what I had expected.

But the amazing thing was that the following morning we were all out to the meeting and as the presence of God filled the meeting hall, I realised that God had not run screaming into the Cosmos in despair, nor was He thinking up ways to zap us into grease balls on the floor. He actually seemed to be smiling! His kids had had a night of fun and hilarity (touches of carnality, it is true) and were now showing even greater passion as they overflowed in adoration and worship.

Those meetings were filled with revelation and inspiration as gifts of the Spirit operated and people stood to share life-changing insights. The level of the word of prophecy being shared was truly remarkable. The fellowship and love (after the first night!) bonded us together and we were not just members of a Movement but friends and comrades knitted together in a noble cause.

We had lots of meetings like that.

On one occasion, during an extended time of free worship, one of the leaders suddenly slipped out of his seat and into the isle and commenced this amazing Cossack-type dance. His eyes were tightly shut! He weaved amongst people, danced onto the stage and around all the various instruments and singers, and not once opening his eyes. As the music interpreted the dance that God had given him, a great sense of victory and triumph filled the air and the praise went into a crescendo. People were greatly touched and set free by the Holy Spirit. He never did open those eyes until after the worship. It truly was a God-given moment of visitation.

The sad thing was, that after a few of those meetings of sovereign intervention, misguided zeal caused us to try and reproduce it and bottle it. There were even 'classes' to train in 'dancing in the spirit'. That was a mistake, I believe. If God did it sovereignly without our help when He obviously wanted to, why then did we think He would need us to perfect with human technique that which was intended to be a demonstration of the miraculous? We would do well to learn that today as He continues to grant us such times of unique and individual visitation.

Those early days were raw. We had no excellence of music, no understanding of leadership principles in books not yet written, and no latest star to come and enthral us with mind-boggling new concepts of how to do church better. All we had was a love for God, a love for each other, and a love for the lost. Strangely, it really did seem enough.

I miss those days.

I thank the Lord for all of the enlightenment of recent decades and the wonderful God-given churches and ministries of a global nature that have brought us so much more understanding of God and His ways. I rejoice over that and have no criticism of it. My only regret is that somehow, along the way, we seem to have lost something of that raw, abandoned, first love spirit of conquest that so motivated our fathers to blaze the trails and forge the Jordan. Perhaps we could all take a moment to ask our King for a renewal of that zeal.

As I was in the middle of writing this particular chapter, my son Aaron, reminded me of another story.

We were living on the church property and a short distance down the road, there was a motorbike gang's headquarters which was heavily fortified with 8 feet high corrugated iron fence and solid steel gates.

One night, when they had obviously been having a party, the volume of their music and celebrating became too loud to bear. With my entire family uttering their fervent protests, I strode down the road to confront them. As I banged on that high steel gate, reality began to dawn on me but it was too late! As the gates swung open, my gaze was jerked upwards to behold this large towering ape-like creature covered in tattoos.

I proceeded to inform him that none of us could sleep due to the loudness of the music and then asked him to please turn it down!

As I now contemplated my early entrance into Heaven, he suddenly burst out laughing and invited me in. He then proceeded to call out to his fellow gang members with, "This guy has got the nerve (he used a different term) to ask us to turn down our music!" As I waited for the machetes and clubs, I found to my astonishment that they too thought it was extremely funny. They invited me to stay and have a drink!

I declined the drink and excused myself with a profound sense of awe that I was still alive. And yes, they did turn down the music!

As I write this, I am a 65 year old grandfather of 6, but I can honestly say that I have never felt more alive, more inspired, more invigorated, more pulsating with vision and a sense of divine commission, in my entire life! If you are in your more mature years, then remember Caleb and re-enlist as God's frontline warriors. You are at the stage when you have the most to give, and there is simply no place for retirement in the Kingdom.

Were those early pioneer days a little rough at the edges? Were there times when we turned God's hair grey? Of that, there is no doubt. But they were also real, filled with passion and 'walking on water' experiences. We were filled with an acute sense of dependence upon God's help and interventions. We were raw, but we were alive!

Chapter Thirteen

SEIZE THE MOMENT

The church began to grow as God found courageous souls not daunted by the prospect of having a 25 year old greenhorn as their senior minister. They came from all walks of life and for various reasons, but they were all filled with an unreasonable faith that God could take this Adullam Cave band of inexperienced raw recruits, and forge something for His honour out of our gathering together.

There were those disillusioned by a sad church experience, those coming to Christ for the first time and those who simply came because "God spoke to them". Each of them brought us great joy as

Margaret and I came to love them as family.

One of the most memorable moments was late one night when we heard banging on the door. As I opened it, I was confronted by a young man who was obviously distraught, who simply declared, "I'm Ned!" He then said that he and his mother had attended some of our services the previous year, and he had come to tell me that his mother had just died. Her last wish was that "Pastor David come and speak to all the relatives when I go".

As her last wish was held in great honour (they were a Maori family), they had dutifully gathered all the relatives (not Christians) around the body, and had sent Ned to come and get me. I was both excited by such an opportunity and scared silly at the same time. What on earth would I say or do? I had no experience in such things and knew nothing of the Maori protocol. I had images of me saying something that immediately offended them all without even knowing it. I cried out to Father and believed for the Holy Spirit to put the right words in my mouth.

As I got there, I felt God's presence and I began to share. I really have no recollection of what I said - it was all a bit of a blur. It was as if I was watching the whole thing while the Holy Spirit used my mouth to say whatever He wanted to. The result was not immediate but overwhelming when it came.

First it was Ned, and then his family members. Then it was his brother, and then his family. Then it was a cousin, who was the principal of the local Intermediate College, and his family. One by one they came to acknowledge Christ as Saviour and crown Him King. I grew to expect the telephone to ring and another family member to be on the other end asking me to come around and pray for them to find Jesus. Husbands and wives would kneel in their lounge and, with tears flowing, were wonderfully born again and filled with His love. We were having our very own mini revival and it was awesome.

I wonder what would have happened if I had thought about the inconvenience of being hauled out of bed in the middle of the night, or had asked for time to consider it because of insecurity about what to do or say. I wonder what would have happened if Ned had found himself trying to book an appointment through my personal assistant. I wonder what amazing and miraculous events have come so close to breaking in upon us but were never realised because we paused to consider the convenience of such an event at that time.

Ned and his family are still in that same local church today, nearly 30 years later.

Then there was the time when, at some ungodly hour of the night, four young ladies in their early twenties banged on our door. As I was about to tell them that they had obviously got the wrong address, one of them asked the question, "Can we find God here?"

They not only encountered God's redeeming love that night but went on to become wonderful friends and members of our congregation. One of them eventually became my church secretary for a while and we maintain a great friendship to this day.

If there is one thing that such events have taught me, it is to 'seize the moment'. The truth is that opportunities for extraordinary things seldom ever come at convenient times. There are simply times when God bursts in upon our schedules and says, *"Do it!"*

I have battled over the years with procrastination and found it to be a formidable foe. Why? Because it can disguise itself as 'being careful' or 'thinking the matter through' or 'not being too hasty'. It can almost seem the rational, logical and reasonable thing to 'chew the fat' a while before acting. In the majority of occasions all of these responses are, in fact, the wise and sane procedure involved with all good decision-making. But what about those times when God just says, *"Do it!"* For example, *"Go in and possess the land"* to Joshua, or

"Come!" to Peter. Such times are not an invitation for a discussion but rather, they are commands.

When the will of God is clear and there is no evidence to the contra, these are the moments when we simply need to act.

I think of the story about Elijah in 1 Kings 18:20-24, where he had to confront 450 of Baal's prophets and an antagonistic king. Nothing about those odds seemed attractive but the situation demanded that somebody do something about it. There has to come that moment when **analysis** of what needs to be done is translated into **doing** what needs to be done.

Elijah could have been like thousands of Christians today, who are contented to sit in the armchairs of their own comfort and security. All the while, they make declarations of what is not being done and what should be done, but they themselves do nothing. There comes a time for every one of us when we need to do something more than just correctly analyse what needs to be done. We need to commit to doing something about it.

In verse 21 of that chapter, we read: *And Elijah came to all the people, and said, "How long will you falter between two opinions? If the LORD is God, follow Him; but if Baal, follow him." But the people answered him not a word.*

They didn't answer him because they were: (a) convicted in their hearts, and (b) not willing to take the course of action that agreeing with him would have demanded of them. They wanted the decision to be made for them. They wanted someone else to take the risk and pay the price before they would consider jumping on board with such a faith venture. If Elijah survived the exercise, then all would be cool. If he died, then they had successfully kept themselves out of it. Intimidated souls still live that way. It has always been so.

Those who gathered in that school hall in 1974 were certainly not that way minded. They had a deep conviction that they had heard from God and that their trust in Him would not be found wanting. I owe them so much, those wonderful ground-breaking people who dared to stand alongside us before any evidence of success began to show itself.

There are so many Christians today whose lives are marking time. They say it is because God hasn't given them something awesome to do. But God is saying it is because that which He has already given them to do has never been fully embraced, the issue has never been settled, the decision never fully made.

Or maybe it is because when He presented them with their opportunity, they failed to seize the moment but rather chose to meditate and think on it until their good sound logic finally argued them out of it. Indecision is a paralysis of the soul. It leads to frustration, disillusionment, self-anger and unhealthy attitudes towards others. Indecision is a torment. It leaves us vulnerable to attacks of unbelief, anxiety and suspicion of others.

More wars have been lost through indecision than anything else; business opportunities have been lost; potential achievements never realised.

Indecision is a paralysis, and while we are in that state of paralysis our adversary comes with his alternative suggestions which are often more enticing. Many a Christian has ended up wandering in the wilderness for years because they failed to seize the moment of God-given opportunity.

Friends, I am not advocating irresponsible prayer-less behaviour, but I am saying that there are times when the window for our obedience is sometimes incredibly brief which then demands an instant act of trust as we step out of the boat.

YOU DID *What?!*

I am reminded of a story which has been told about Winston Churchill and Lady Astor. They apparently loathed each other and all precautions were taken to ensure that they were not invited to the same functions. However, on this one occasion, that is exactly what happened and Lady Astor got there first. As Winston walked in, she approached him and in an attempt to embarrass him in front of some ambassador, declared, "If you, Sir, were my husband, I would lace your coffee with poison." Winston, without batting an eyelid, replied, "Madam, if you were my wife, I'd drink it!" Winston knew how to seize the moment!

Then consider the Allied armies awaiting the moment to take back Europe from Hitler. The weather was so bad that an invasion was impossible and the German army was content in that knowledge. Then a meteorologist spotted a small break in the weather conditions which would permit the armada to get across the English Channel. The weather window for the invasion of Europe was just a few hours but that was all that was needed. Eisenhower and Churchill talked for just a few moments (that was all they had), and a decision was made that changed the course of history and liberated millions of people. Together, they seized the moment.

Looking back on my journey, there have been many times when what was needed were days of prayer and seeking God. There have also been those times when, out of walking daily in intimacy with His heart, I heard that unmistakable voice spoken too clearly to be misunderstood or disobeyed. Times of witnessing to people on the plane, times of giving finance to one in need, times of ringing someone on the phone, times of dropping all the admin duties and finding a solitary place to come aside with Him.

Chapter Fourteen

TEARS AND TRIUMPH

There have been many times over the years when circumstances have had Margaret and I bewildered and, initially in anguish of heart.

On one such occasion, not long after we started in Manurewa, we noticed that our middle child, Steve, then at 6 weeks of age, had an obvious eye defect. His eyes would be forever floating, trying to latch on to something upon which to focus and would also flicker up and down very rapidly. We took him to be examined by an eye specialist.

We were initially told that he was blind. We were devastated and cried out to the Lord for understanding and felt not to accept this condition. We gathered people around and we prayed and anointed him with oil, believing for a divine intervention.

When we had him re-examined, the specialist informed us that there must have been a mistake in the earlier diagnosis as Steve was not blind, but did have an incurable defect that would eventually render him blind. We were to accept this and adjust as his blindness was certain. We were instructed to enrol him in the Homai College for the Blind, so that at an early age he could commence education for his life of inevitable blindness. As young parents, we had so many questions but could not find it in ourselves to give up hope. We shared it with relatives and friends who joined us in prayer and believing.

Some months later, we were attending a camp at Snell's Beach which was north of Auckland, with a visiting evangelist from Australia. Steve's eyes were still showing the same frantic movement, forever searching for something to focus on. At one of the meetings, we made the decision to have Steve prayed for by this evangelist. There was a great sense of faith due to some of the other miracles which had taken place, and we believed again for God's power to be demonstrated. Almost immediately the flickering started to slow down and as we watched over the next few months, every day showed slight improvement. We had had our miracle!

For reasons best known to Father, Steve's eyes were never 100% healed and he remains with some vision impairment today. However, he drives a car, ministers internationally and plays competitive indoor soccer! Not bad for someone who is supposed to be blind!

Why not a full and complete healing? We really do not know. But we are eternally grateful for the quality of life that Steve enjoys, and the zeal and passion with which he embraces it. Most of us walk through life with one form of a 'limp' or another; Steve's is a physical one. Do we believe that he will yet receive full sight? We still contend for that but do not live a life controlled by that expectation. There is simply too much to be grateful for and too much which can be achieved with or without that outcome. Steve is living life to the max, and so are we.

Other events have not finished with such an intervention.

One young lady, who was very close to us as a family and often looked after our children, died of cancer. That was so very hard to take at the time and even harder to explain to our young children who had so many questions.

Then there was the time that Brian died at just 32 years of age.

Brian was my best friend and married to Margaret's sister, Jocelyn. We were inseparable as two couples, and Brian and I were like David and Jonathan. When they went to the Philippines as missionaries, we missed them deeply but reassured ourselves that we could still see them on days of furlough, or if we visited them over there. On the mission field, they were a long way away but it wasn't final. From the mission field, Brian could always come home.

Their days there were incredibly fruitful but often extremely hard, especially when they lost their baby. Then they received an invitation to come back and pastor the church on the North Shore of Auckland. This was the church which had originally sent us all out into ministry. The pastor was going overseas and Brian was to take over as Senior Minister. We were overjoyed to all be in the same city again and anticipated some amazing times of fun and friendship.

Initially, Brian ministered powerfully and that church experienced the beautiful touch of the Master through his compassionate pastor's heart. They were great days.

Then Brian was diagnosed with cancer. It was rapid and unrelenting, and I feel it serves no end in this book to relive the week to week pain of that time. Sufficient to say that it was incredibly hard for us all who loved him as well as loved Jocelyn and the boys. So many tears were shed as we prayed and believed, and prayed again and again, and yet again. Our prayer and faith were daily and our claiming of Scriptures was as unrelenting as the foe itself.

Until the very end, I believed that God was going to miraculously heal Brian. Margaret and I moved into the hospital for the last two weeks and stayed in a room adjacent to his (as did Jocelyn). Day after day, we confessed life to him and watched as this selfless man of God thought constantly about others and sought only to minister grace and love to all who were around him. The memory of his Christlikeness still impacts me today.

Then, finally, the Lord took him to be with Himself.

As I walked out into the cold and wet car park that night, I wept in sorrow, already missing the one person on the planet I loved second only to my wife and children. How desperately I missed him. I still do today. He was more than a friend. He was my confidant, the one with whom I could be 100% real, the one who could rebuke me and never leave a scar, the one who constantly encouraged me and told me I could overcome when things seemed overwhelming. He was my chief example of what living a godly, selfless life was all about, my inspiration and goad to be more like Jesus by being more like him.

I walked out of that hospital under a bleak and overcast sky and I made a vow that night. I told the Lord that I did not know how long He would give me, but every moment of it would be spent to honour Him. Brian's life had left such an impression, such an impact, that I just wanted to pick up that baton and touch others as he had touched me. Hundreds of others were impacted the same way.

In Auckland, at his memorial service, approximately (details a little foggy as it was over 30 years ago) 50 young men and women stood to give their lives for ministry service. In Christchurch, at another memorial service for him, approximately 150 stood for commitment to Christian ministry. Hundreds of lives were impacted and changed forever. I have thought many times about the Scripture verse, *Unless a kernel of wheat falls to the ground and dies, it remains only a single seed. But if it dies, it produces many seeds* [see John 12:24]. This was abundantly so with Brian's promotion to glory.

Do I have a revelation of why? Not really. For the most part I believe it was connected with the above Scripture, and in part for reasons best known to the Lord, which I will find out one day as I meet Him and renew my friendship with Brian. But this thing I do know: there was, and is, a wonderful provision of God's grace at such times; and the witness and eternal fruit of Brian's life and death achieved an eternal purpose which could not be achieved any other way.

To live life long but to live it without honour or eternal significance is a tragedy. Length of days is not necessarily a measuring rod of a life well lived. Some of the greatest heroes of the faith over the ages have died relatively young. It has been well said that it is not when a man dies but how he lives that is important. Not the condition of the body or the environment, but the internal state, the attitudes and the nobility of the heart. To live with dishonour is not to have lived at all, but to die with honour after having served Christ and one's friends selflessly, is to have lived to the applause of Heaven and the gratitude of your peers.

Jesus and Brian lived about the same amount of time on planet earth and both magnificently achieved their God-given commission. I am empowered by their example. I am determined to honour Brian's memory by living life as he would be living it now if he had remained with us: loving people, caring for others in their times of pain, and fully focussed on serving the King and His 'cause'. Life is too short to live it any other way.

Brian's life was short, but his life was a triumph.

Chapter Fifteen

GENTLE STEEL, ELISHA AND COMPASSIONATE GRIT

The sweat, the tears, the sucking in of air, the gruntin g, the emotional trauma, the sleepless night and the involvement of hospital staff was just so intense. And that was just me! Margaret was valiantly bringing into this world our first child.

Rachael from birth was the most beautiful and wonderful gift to Margaret and myself. Her disposition was gentle and compliant and yet she had an inner strength that was to show itself in later years. In recent years, as a missionary in Africa with her husband and two sons, she has had to draw on that inner strength time and again.

YOU DID What?!

With great joy, we remember Rachael accepting Jesus as her Lord and Saviour at an early age and almost immediately beginning to dream of one day serving the Lord in some missionary capacity. This led to an involvement in a short-term team to Fiji in her late teens and another one to Hong Kong and China at the age of 21.

Always a little shy and uncertain of the unknown, Rachael's humility and conservative perception of herself made it more difficult for her to reach out and tackle new challenges head on. However, whenever encouraged to do so, she would overcome and dare to believe that what her Dad and Mum were telling her was in fact the truth. Without a natural disposition of daring, she would step out in faith, relying on the Holy Spirit each time.

I once heard a Vietnam War veteran, winner of numerous awards for bravery, make this statement: "Courage is not the absence of fear; it is the conquering of that fear with a sense of responsibility that is greater than one's fear." Whenever I think of that statement, I think of Rachael. For someone whose disposition is to be shy and cautious, she has become a wonderful wife, devoted mother, and lady of great faith who has served beside her husband in Tanzania and Ethiopia for more than 11 years. (They are now back in Melbourne as a family.)

Rachael has learnt to teach English as a second language, learnt to live in the most difficult of circumstances, adapted to a life often without water or electricity for hours or days at a time, battled demonic forces, overcome depression, and emerged as an overcomer. Words cannot describe how much I love and admire her.

I remember well the day that God brought Steve, her husband, into her life. Bearing in mind that she was 26 at the time, he could not believe that she would not go out on a date without him first asking her father's permission!

All Steve had seen of me, at that time, was this fiery preacher declaring hot rhetoric from the pulpit. He was understandably a little awkward about our getting together. I should have swiftly put his fears at ease and hurried to reassure him, but this 6'4" giant wanted to date my daughter and possibly go on to marry her! My daughter! My only daughter!! Putting him at ease was the furthest thing from my mind.

I picked him up and we drove to a nearby park. As beads of sweat began to break out upon his brow and his upper lip, I proceeded to interrogate this potential son-in-law. It was a blend of intense prophet, protective father, and Irish rhetoric and ... oh yes, listening too, of course!

As I saw that the daunting prospect of having me as his father-in-law had numbed his senses and reduced his kneecaps to jelly, I was surprised, but deeply impressed, to hear him prevail again in his request to start dating my daughter. Today, I thank the Lord for giving Rachael such a loving husband and a devoted father to my grandsons, Sean and Nathan.

Sean and Nathan totally adapted to life in Africa and their grandparents were forever scheming (and praying too) to find ways to see them on an annual basis. It is now wonderful to have them live only minutes away. They are great kids and live their lives like their diet is one of rocket fuel and hot chillies!

Our second child is Stephen, or Steve as he is better known.

Steve was also compliant as a child and soft of nature. However, his determination and courage were seen at an early age as we discovered that he had severe sight impairment. This led to restricted activities such as sport, yet he flung himself into athletics. He figured that as long as he could see some track in front of him, he had a good chance of winning the race!

Although I knew of his struggle through those teenage years, his sensitive responsive nature had a hunger for God. He also discovered in those years that God had graced him with an ability to play the piano and other instruments. While still a teenager, he began to play in our Sunday services and soon emerged as a worship leader.

I remember him coming home after a particularly difficult day at high school, playing the piano and worshipping God in our basement with such vigour that he broke one of the strings! In fact, over the years, he broke more than one of those strings.

When we arrived in Australia at Waverley Christian Fellowship (detailed in a later chapter), Steve's capacity to lead other people into genuine worship became apparent, and he was often asked to lead worship in the Sunday services.

His diligence empowered him to rise from factory worker to State Purchasing Manager for a large company in a relatively short time, and his witness was such that he still has good relationships with many in that company to this very day.

Steve went on to be an associate pastor in a new church plant for nearly 7 years, and then some 6 years ago joined my own team as a prophet. His ministry is now well received throughout the nation and overseas and he is a wonderful strength to me personally. I will share more about that later.

Another thing that happened to Steve, upon his arrival in Australia, was that he noticed this young solo mother with a little baby. To be more accurate, he noticed the baby first. Upon falling in love with the baby, he discovered the mother. Sally was God's stroke of creative genius for Steve. With Steve's passion for the prophetic and zealous fervour (chip off the old block), he needed someone who actually knew about the practical everyday issues of life. They really were opposites in so many areas of life and yet God drew them together like two magnets.

They married, and today Sally is the dynamic founder and leader of Angel Light Link, a Christian organisation dedicated to helping young teenage girls going through challenges in life. It would be also true to say that Sally has had an enormous impact on our family. Her wisdom and counsel has touched every member of our extended family and I am incredibly grateful for God gifting her to us. They have two delightful teenage daughters, Kirrily and Brianna, who make our hearts so very proud. The great miracle is that the girls can still communicate intelligently with their utterly 'ancient' grandparents and seem to truly enjoy doing so. For me, that is (as they say it), really cool!

Our third child was a coiled ball of energy named Aaron. It seemed from birth his spirit of adventure propelled him to push the limits and to pursue adventure. Bruises and scars gave testimony to the fact that 'the safe life' was not going to be his option.

One of my early recollections of Aaron was when he was five years old and we were having our first visit to Disneyland in California. It was in the middle of a heat wave, and we had been in the park for 12 straight hours. As the rest of us staggered exhausted across the car park, Aaron was doing flips and demanding that we go in for another 12 hours!

Of all his admirable traits, none stand out greater than his sheer grit. An example was when, in his early teens, he had compassion on an elderly lady down the street and took our lawnmower to mow her lawns for her. On the way back, he was attacked by some large vicious dogs that proceeded to maul him and ripped open his leg. He fought off the dogs and managed to stagger his way back towards our home, but only to remember halfway home that he had left the lawn mower behind. He then went back to get the lawnmower and pushed it the whole way back into our driveway! Upon seeing my shock and horror as I viewed the blood and gore that used to be his leg, he proceeded to admonish me with the statement: "Now Dad, don't do anything stupid. I'm going to need your help with this!"

Not only did that incident become the first of many that showed his incredible capacity to handle pain and persevere through difficulty, but was also an early demonstration of his caring and compassionate nature when seeing people in genuine need. Over the years I have seen him at many times lay aside his own personal needs to minister help, comfort and counsel to those going through difficulty. He is simply one of the most selfless and pastorally-minded people I have ever met. His insight into the hurt and trauma that people experience has led him to giving words of wisdom to us all on many an occasion.

Then there was the day where Margaret and I were called in to the hospital. Aaron had had an accident.

While building a house, Aaron had shot himself through the leg with a heavy duty nail gun! When we arrived, we saw that it was even worse than we had thought. The nail was the size of a spike and was protruding out the front and the back of his leg immediately above the kneecap. The surgeon was trying to get Aaron to agree to being put to sleep while the removal of the nail took place. He assured us that our son was in agony. Aaron's response was uniquely what we had grown to expect from him: "Are you kidding? How many times are we going to get to see something like this? Somebody get a camera!" Life with Aaron has never been boring.

Aaron's world was one of shooting wild things in the bush, gaining scars through constant incidents of impact, living life in the rough and raw, and being bewildered by those more timid mortals who enjoyed classical music. That is until God couldn't contain His sense of humour and one day introduced him to Tracie.

Tracie was petite, refined, and loved the theatre!

It simply had to be a miracle of God. And it was. He was once again demonstrating that often the strongest marriages emerge from two total opposites being placed together.

It is amazing - Tracie now goes camping and Aaron goes to the theatre and enjoys "Les Miserables". They have an incredible bond that has taken them through some huge challenges in life; challenges which would have destroyed most people, but they emerged stronger than ever. God has blessed them (and us!) with their children, Hannah and Liam, who are a constant delight. Hannah takes after Tracie and is a beautiful young lady. Liam is like we remember Aaron at that age - a tireless tornado of energy and life.

The Bible says that *children are the heritage of the Lord* [see Psalm 127:3]. As I know this to be true, I am overwhelmed with gratitude that the Lord has not only given Margaret and myself three wonderful children, but that they have all grown into adulthood still loving God and their parents. Our grandchildren are all awesome and it is a priceless gift that we all have a deep love for each other and are great friends.

Is this to say that there have not been times of great trauma? Of course not! In common with all parents, Margaret and I have known what it is to wrestle with God for our children, and weep secretly in the private place. Our children have not been perfect, and neither have we been as parents. However, the previous paragraph is true, and the persistence of God's prevailing grace has been the key. The strength of our wider family bond today is not due to perfect people, nor perfect parenting; but entirely on God's faithfulness and wisdom that came in response to our crying out to Him for it. The result was the discovery of principles that empowered us to parent beyond our natural capacity to do so.

Perhaps there are those reading this book that are facing deep challenges within their family relationships. Let me assure you that it's never too late, and that God is eager to come to your aid even as you ask Him to. Remember, He knows what it is like to be a father.

Chapter Sixteen

CLAIMING DIRT AND DREAMING BIG

It was 1980 and it was time for a major challenge in faith.

When you have a congregation of barely 70 people and the offerings are not sufficient to cover existing costs so that you are praying for miracles every week just to put bread on the table, the thought of a building programme is like building a space station on Mars.

One day, while out driving, I noticed this great piece of land immediately around the corner from my house. It was owned by Universal Homes who had built our own home. I felt that God was saying to build a church on that piece of land but could see no way in which such a thing could be possible.

Margaret and I prayed it through and then submitted it to our church leadership team. We all got a witness in our hearts that such indeed was the intention of God for that piece of land. I approached Universal Homes and awaited their response.

Initially, they shared the impossibility of such a thing occurring, as the land was in fact five house blocks (Kiwis call them 'sections'), and they had special designs for the homes that were to go on there. It was prime land and maybe they could discuss something else with us. Our response was gracious but definite - that was the piece of land. The owner of Universal Homes was a Christian businessman named Bill Subritzky and he agreed to pray about it. The result was that, not only did they sell us the land, but they did so at a fraction of its true value. The miracle had commenced.

The following is an article in the Courier Newspaper of that day. Please bear in mind that it was 1980 and the value of the dollar in those days. The price of a house and land package back then was about $20,000. A huge salary was $100 a week! Most people were earning a fraction of that. So you can multiply the figures below by almost fifteen times to get an accurate picture in today's terms.

Article in "Courier" (NZ Newspaper), Saturday September 13, 1980:

New Life Centre Opens in Manurewa
A dream becomes a reality

> When Pastor David McCracken and his wife, Margaret, commenced at New Life Centre in October 1973 with only 9 adults (then known as South Auckland Faith Centre), there was a big dream and an unshakeable confidence in their God ... and very

little else!

As people began to respond to the simple declaration of God's love, there gathered a small congregation who decided there was a need for a non-denominational chapel and counselling centre in the Manurewa West area. Almost immediately, they were able to secure the land from Universal Homes for an unbelievable sum of $500 deposit. The little handful met together and in the offering that next Sunday there came in $503! They were on their way. Through a series of exciting "faith stories" this small congregation continued to pay off the land until the full $18,750 was paid in full.

During the next six years there were many times when their faith was severely tested as they endeavoured to see the "dream" become a reality. The struggle to be accepted; the increasing financial hurdles; the enormity of human need around them; constant need to shift premises; these things presented them with continual challenges. Through those years they proved the great faithfulness of their God. "The Lord has been so good to us" is a term frequently heard. In fact, there is an overwhelming sense of appreciation and gratitude of the Lord for what has been achieved. Pastor McCracken and his wife feel that being able to play a part in it all has been a privilege and see no way anyone other than the Lord can claim it as "their work".

Then came the challenge to build itself. After many sets of plans had been discussed, they finally settled on a Modulock structure for practicability. Construction started in February 1980 and their confidence in God's provision and the day of miracles had to now find new heights. What makes the story remarkable is throughout this time the priority of the fellowship was never the building itself but most definitely that of people. With a community aid team and marriage counsellors aiding Pastor McCracken and his wife, this congregation has worked to meet the needs of the community about them. This has required (on occasions) to give very substantial financial aid to families in need.

With a full-time missionary in the Philippines and support being given to those in need locally, the financial turnover needed to run the fellowship's activities was always more than seemingly possible. Their very firm declaration is they have been only able to continue by God's own miraculous supply.

With five moves in the previous 18 months, it was with great joy they finally commenced services in their own building on June 22, 1980. Since that time they have been endeavouring to finish bits and pieces as well as find the necessary finance to pay for the building. Overall, there has been a total in excess of $50,000 given toward the project (including the land). All but $1000 has come via their own giving as "God supplied miraculously". With an outstanding $75,000 they will obviously need a few miracles yet to come.

Pastor McCracken is determined that the building should be debt-free as soon as possible, so that the cash-flow in the fellowship can be spent entirely on the needs of people. They envisage full time counselling services, and increase in youth work, a work with solo parents, children's work, welfare working increasing; along with normally accepted aspects of congregational life.

Above all, the desire is to be more able to effectively demonstrate the "love of God in Jesus Christ" to those about them. The warmth and love that binds them together, they say, can "only be found as God places His love in your heart". It is this love and obvious reality of their faith that has caused them to touch many families in their area.

We were a church of middle and low income families and the challenge that this project presented financially was absolutely huge. Let me remind you again that it was 1980 when $1000 was a gigantic amount of money, and we still had a very small congregation of less than 70 people. We had experienced a miracle with the land but now needed daily miracles to keep going forward. We had no millionaires and outside help was not in the offering. We sought God as to how He was to supply.

It is true that God could have supplied the entire amount with a flicker of His eyeball (He has done so since on many an occasion), but far greater than the provision were the lessons He wanted to teach us. Dependence upon His miraculous provision was but one principle; sacrifice was another.

In the middle of the building project, Margaret and I felt stirred to sacrifice financially and lead the way by example. After prayer, we both felt that the home the Lord gave us was part of the answer and agreed to sell it, putting the bulk of the equity into the building fund. We were back to renting (for another 8 years) but excited that the 'pioneering spirit' was still alive. Others followed suit and made incredible sacrifices of various capital items, including three people who also donated the proceeds from selling their homes. It was a time of excitement and zeal, and reminded us of the Book of Acts where *they sold all and placed it at the Apostles' feet* [see Acts 4:37].

It was a season of deliberate purpose as God forged in us principles and a value system that were to stay with us throughout our ministry life. I am not suggesting that every leader should do what we did, but I am saying that every leader should lead by example and not expect sacrifice from their people that they are not first willing to embrace.

Perhaps the most powerful and releasing thing that this season achieved in Margaret and myself, was being released from making the gaining of financial independence and capital gain a priority. We have seen so many over the years who have allowed this legitimate pursuit to gain such a dominion in them, that it has eclipsed the greater call of God in their lives. We have proven, again and again, that if one *puts first the Kingdom of God, all things shall be added to them* [see Matthew 6:33]. From that day to today, we have not made a priority of pursuing capital gain and dwellings, and yet live in a beautiful home on an idyllic one acre property ideally suited to our personal and ministry needs. God is no man's debtor. We have learnt that if we build His house, He will look after ours.

Once the building was completed, we began services and then a Christian school. They were wonderful and exciting days and the church grew with new people being added constantly.

Chapter Seventeen

VALUES AND THE BETRAYAL OF EGGS

The era in which Margaret and I got married was a hazardous one for the family of those in ministry. There were tales of strained marriages, hurt or rebellious children, and of the need to see this as one of the more demanding price tags placed upon the commitment of those in ministry.

This was the generation of 'P.K.s' (Preachers' Kids). Although there were definite exceptions, this was one of the more alarming challenges for those called to take up the full-time mantle.

We were determined that it would not be so for our own marriage and children. We sought God for the answers.

It was obvious that there would be many occasions in which the time allotted to family would come under assault. It was also obvious that a strong value system was necessary. The value system that we felt to be biblical was as follows: God first, our marriage second, our children third, and the work of the ministry fourth. We decided to reject the old concept that the work of the ministry had to come first, second and third.

Firmly believing that this value system was born in our hearts by the Lord, we planned our lives accordingly. On more than one occasion, it was strongly challenged.

In 1980, with the building completed and the church growing, it was decided that I should accept an invitation from an apostle in the USA (Dick Benjamin) to minister in his movement of churches. I was informed that I was to come as a prophet bringing the 'Word of the Lord', and that the opportunities would necessitate a considerable amount of time. It turned out to be about 4½ months.

It was a wonderful opportunity to minister into a large group of churches but the invitation only covered my expenses. Love offerings and honorariums in those days often barely covered the airfare, let alone any other expenses. This was a not to be missed opportunity but one which directly confronted my value system. To be away months from my wife and children was an obvious violation of the commitment we had made. Did this mean that the invitation was not God's will? We prayed concerning the matter.

We came to the conclusion that this was indeed what God was asking of us at that time, which left us with only one conclusion - we were all to go together. It was 'walking on water' time again. With our house gone (into our church building programme) and very little money in the bank, we were faced with an absolute impossibility.

As Margaret and I had made a commitment that the work of the ministry would never take priority over the family (a value that we have held to for 40 years now), this meant that for me to take up this invitation, I would have to take the entire family with me. This, of course, meant 5 airfares instead of one, 5 times the food, increased accommodation and numerous other considerations. In addition, it would mean that Margaret would have to homeschool the children for the duration of the journey. The challenges seemed gigantic!

We sold whatever items we did not essentially need and believed God for the rest. The airfares came in and we flew out with a few dollars to see us through the first few days until the first love offering. I could feel the thin ice cracking but reminded myself that Peter had no ice at all. The responsibility of the children and Margaret was very real, but so too, the deep inner knowing that this was yet another season of discovering God's greatness that was vital for who He was making us to be. Friends, all of life is that way if you can but recognise it.

Here's where it got hairy.

Have you ever discovered that when God wants you dependent upon Him, He is incredibly thorough in His removing of all other sources of security? Well, it's true!

We stopped over in Hawaii on the way to Los Angeles. and ministered at a local church there. The following morning the pastor 'took' us all out for brunch at a nice local restaurant. To my surprise, he had invited others along as well which made quite a good sized group of us. I ordered something called "Eggs Benedict" which immediately explained why the name "Benedict" today is associated with betrayal. It was gooey, under-cooked eggs on a muffin soaked in butter, topped with what felt like melted cheese and cream. My stomach and my mind competed for which one would throw up first. (I have since had Eggs Benedict that was actually quite pleasant, but these had obviously been made by a sadist whose only avenue for venting on the human race was by his cooking.)

But the real shock was what then followed.

At the conclusion of the meal, I casually made this remark to the pastor, "Would you like me to help you with this?" (Not for one minute thinking that he would accept my offer as I was his guest!) In reality, it was a polite and appropriate way to say, "I do not take your kindness for granted and am willing to contribute some small amount towards it."
Without hesitation, he said, "Why, thank you!", and handed me the entire bill before leading the group out of the restaurant! I was shocked! Almost the full amount of our desperately needed love offering had been blown on our first morning's breakfast.

"Was this going to be normal?"
"Is this how they test you over here?"
"How are we ever going to get enough to travel and live?"
"God, help!"
These thoughts flooded into my mind as I tried to outwardly appear as if all had been anticipated and I was taking it in my stride.

God was simply reminding us that He was our Provider and that even love offerings can evaporate if we come to depend on them. He and He alone is our Provider. That was, to this very day, the last time such an event has occurred on a ministry trip. Once was enough for Father to get the point across.

I also learnt never again to be insincere with statements about money and who pays at the restaurant! I have learnt to say what I mean and mean what I say.

The remainder of that trip was one of constant provision. Day by day, church by church, collective love offerings and individual gifts just kept us always one step ahead. It was a journey of faith but one on which our children learned to trust the faithfulness of a God who is never late; often in the nick of time (11:59), but never late.

As that trip drew toward a close, God began to supply an excess of what we actually needed and we announced to the children that we were all off to Disneyland. What an experience that was! It was a Californian heatwave, and we were one of the first to arrive that day and one of the last to leave. Coming from New Zealand, we had never seen anything like it. The kids decided that serving God and being the children of a minister were not really that bad.

One of the lasting images I have from that particular occasion is of our younger son, Aaron, doing flips in the car park as the rest of us staggered in exhaustion towards the car. (Oh yes, I've mentioned that already. Shows you how vivid a memory it is!)

Those were invaluable memories and lessons in God's faithfulness that would never have taken place had it not been for our commitment to the value system that God had given us.

Another such occasion was when our middle child, Steve, was in his mid-teens. I was away ministering in Adelaide, South Australia, and was due to fly to Melbourne to have further meetings there. One day the phone rang and Steve was explaining to me that he had been falsely accused of an issue and that the processing of it was particularly painful. It was clear that he was deeply affected by this and after giving him some fatherly counsel, I assured him that I would be praying for him.

Getting off the phone, I was reminded of my value system. I must stress that this was not a superficial issue but one of substantial pressure and conflict. As I prayed, I realised that my love for Steve and my commitment to my value system demanded of me that I return home. I was faced with the dilemma of how this balanced with my integrity concerning the meetings I had committed to speak at in Melbourne.

My prayer went something like this: "Lord, You know that the value system You gave me demands this action from me now. But You also made me a man of integrity. In Your foreknowledge, You must have known that this decision would have to be made and therefore You must know who it is who must replace me for those meetings in Melbourne." Instantly, the name 'Kevin Forlong' came into my mind. I rang Kevin and asked him what he was doing for the following few days and he informed me that he was taking a break. I then told him that he was going to be on a plane to Melbourne! Well, actually, I pleaded and begged him to save my hide.

That church in Melbourne was mightily blessed through Kevin's ministry, and to this day Steve has never forgotten the moment when I walked through our front door.

I have had similar incidents with Rachael and with Aaron. Only a handful in four decades, but just enough to test the convictions that Margaret and I held, and still hold to this day.

Audacious Faith Adventures in the Life of David McCracken

Top left: Oh, so cute!
Top right: Mum, me, Dad and Tony
            living in England
Middle: Our family in New Zealand
Right: My best impersonation
            of a Maori warrior

YOU DID *What?!*

Top left: Cool dude
Top right: Elvis ... or me?
Above: All grown up!
Right: Suave me - I did mention the 'ego'

Top left: Off to evangelise Fiji with YWAM
Top right: World changers in Fiji
Bottom left: Scorched and barefooted ... loved it!
Bottom right: 21st birthday (with Dad and Mum)

YOU DID What?!

Left: Our wedding day, November 1970
Below: Sealed with a kiss
Bottom: Wedding party

Audacious Faith Adventures in the Life of David McCracken

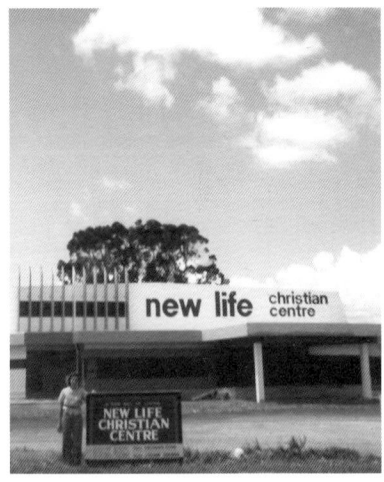

Top left: Pioneering days of Manukau New Life Centre, NZ
Top right: Building a new church
Middle left: Our young family - Rachael, Steve and Aaron
Middle right: The classic pose of yesteryears
Bottom left: First USA trip - love that beard!
Bottom right: Jim and Anneke Shaw

YOU DID What?!

Top left: Immigrating to Australia, 1992
Above: The kids sharing at our combined 50th birthday celebration
Left: On part-time staff at Waverley Christian Fellowship (now CityLife Church)

Top left: Mission trip to Nigeria
Top right: Mission trip to Tanzania
Above: Huge crusade in Tanzania (I am 2nd from right)
Left: Visiting an orphanage in Uganda

YOU DID *What?!*

Top left: Beautiful summer's day, Switzerland
Top right: Next day, after praying for snow!
Middle left: Celebrating 40th wedding anniversary jet-boating in Queenstown, NZ
Middle right: Celebrating 40th wedding anniversary in Wanaka, NZ
Bottom: The McCracken family portrait, 2008

Chapter Eighteen

LET OUT OF PRISON

Upon reaching that first church on mainland USA in 1980, I discovered something quite remarkable was happening. Firstly, I was told absolutely nothing about the church and asked to 'get the mind of God for them' without the intrusion of human understanding. Secondly, in my times of preparation, I began to receive very specific pictures and phrases which I knew had to do with that particular church and its people and vision. It was scary in detail. Thirdly, as I began to minister in the church, an effortless flow of words of knowledge and words of prophecy began, both to individuals and leadership.

This proceeded to be the case in each of the churches we visited, until finally we ended up in Anchorage at the original church out of which the others had been planted. Abbot Loop Christian Center was gigantic! Long before the days of the 'mega church' when a large church was anything over 100, they had a congregation of 1500+ (it was a long time ago and the actual numbers are hazy). Not only was I awed at the privilege of ministering there as such a young man, but the prophetic flow I had been experiencing kicked one notch even higher.

We also saw some remarkable physical healings take place. God had quickened to me the difference between making a petition and declaring a command in the name of the Lord Jesus Christ. The example of Peter at the Gate Beautiful came alive to me, in which no prayer was uttered, only the declaration: *...but what I do have I give you: In the name of Jesus Christ of Nazareth, rise up and walk* [see Acts 3:6]. Again and again I found myself using the phrase, "Now do what you could not do, in Jesus name", and amazing miracles of healing took place. It was an exciting time!

One day over coffee, I asked the Senior Minister, Dick Benjamin, why was it that such a prophetic mantle had come upon me during this visit to his churches. His answer was about to release me from an imprisonment imposed upon me some 5 years previously. I look back on it with great gratitude, knowing that it was such a critical moment in God's purposes.

His answer was, "Their only expectation was for you to minister as a prophet. That is the office and the ministry I told them you carried. We had not asked you to come as a pastor or a teacher, but as a prophet. In receiving you as a prophet, we have gained a 'prophet's reward'." He then went further and challenged me to no longer back away from my calling but to embrace it. I could feel the emotion whelming up from within. This man had no idea the significance of what he was saying and what God was saying to me through him.

Let me take you back 5 years.

Having pioneered and then pastored for a few years as a 'pastor with a prophetic gift', I was awakened one morning with a great urgency to get aside and listen as God had something to say to me. He then took me to Jeremiah chapter one and proceeded to tell me that He had called me to the office of the prophet and that I would minister in that office and calling to the nations.

I was so excited! What wonderful news! I couldn't wait for all my friends and colleagues to celebrate with me. So I did the 'Joseph' thing. I rushed out and told my brethren. Oops!

One must understand that in the mid-70s, the understanding and acceptance of the roles of the apostle and the prophet was nothing like it is today. Back then you were not allowed to pronounce the word "prophet", let alone believe you could be one!

As I shared my exciting news with a senior minister in our Movement, his response was one of shock and rebuke. He could not believe how I had allowed such pride and arrogance into my heart and proceeded to tell me that if I did not meet with God in deep repentance over it, this illusion of grandeur would destroy me and any potential of future acceptance in ministry. He then turned to Margaret and urged her to argue me out of this lunacy and ensure that it did not return.

I was devastated! Not at his response, but at how I could be that deceived and arrogant. Completely broken, I raced home to repent, and begged God to forgive me that I had allowed myself to believe such a thing. It never crossed my mind that this minister may not have been correct in his judgement. After all, he walked with God and was deeply loved and respected.

Over the next 5 years, God would, at various times, endeavour to gain my attention to His calling on my life as a prophet. Each time would result in the most sincere and heart-rending repentance. To me, it was evidence that stinking pride was trying to assail me once again. I so desperately wanted to prove to God and to others that I really was not that proud.

This grew into a deep insecurity in my life which compelled me to forever qualify whatever commission God gave me, with the examination of whether or not it had the potential to make me look 'proud'. Above all, I had to prove my humility if I was to please God and be accepted by my brethren. This led to years of diluting God's directives to me, modifying them to ensure they would not be considered proud in any way. Without knowing it, the quest for humility had replaced my quest for obedience.

I have struggled all of my ministry life to fully overcome the deep scar of intimidation that was etched into my spirit at that time. But the level of obedience and consequent authority that I progressively experienced by His grace in these last three decades, can be traced back to that conversation with Dick.

As Dick continued to speak God's call into my life, I felt like a Gideon, hardly daring to believe it but knowing that it was true. The evidence I had seen in the previous weeks of ministering in the USA had most powerfully confirmed it. I returned to New Zealand a different man, and in those 5 years the acceptance of such a role in the Body of Christ had also changed. Upon beginning to minister in New Zealand on my return, I found those who had been so cautious concerning the prophet's ministry were now much more open and accepting of that role, and my calling in particular. In fact, not long after that, I was asked to be a member of the National Leadership Team of our Movement of Churches. At that time, the youngest to be asked to do so.

Where the words of one man imprisoned the prophetic call within me, the words of another had unlocked the door and set it free. Let us never underestimate the power of our words in the hearts of those who look to us for counsel. It is a great responsibility to ensure that our words support and encourage God's intention in that individual's life.

If you are now wondering about how that trip ended up financially after the 'Eggs Benedict' episode, let me say that it was one wonderfully miraculous provision after the other. The wonderful generosity of the American churches and God's constant 'out of the blue' interventions meant that the entire family came home with a book full of testimonies and our children got to see and experience things very rarely experienced by those their age (or any of us for that matter!).

During those early years when the children were young, we were able to take the entire family to USA for four extended ministry trips and one to Australia. Not once did we have the money to do so when we said yes to God's directives, and not once did we end up in debt as a result. Often without any money in the bank at all (other than for immediate groceries, etc.), we would pray together until we were deeply convinced God had spoken and then go out and book the tickets. Bear in mind that this was not as it is today - the promise of a 'love offering' or 'honorarium' could range anywhere from $50 upwards for a weekend! They were days of radical faith in which God was preparing us for the enormous steps of faith that we now must take as a ministry team. It was then that a critical part of our existing DNA and life message was forged - **Obedience first, miracle second!**

Margaret and I have now travelled to an amazing number of places including Africa, India, Asia and Europe, and many of those completely on faith and obedience. God is so very faithful when we allow Him to be by our obedience.

YOU DID *What?!*

Chapter Nineteen

SPRINKLING SOME SALT

A *hardness born of despair, a drawn look that gripped me as I sped by. It was come and gone in a moment, but one of a multitude that you see each day.*

Margaret has often commented that I seem to study people without knowing I do it. I guess that is so. I just find myself wondering what is behind that countenance; the story, the journey, the struggles of life. Do they have a family? Why the sadness? The weariness in their walk; the way they looked at shop windows with eyes that did not see for their mind was so occupied with some unspoken trauma. I find myself wondering sometimes if that is but a hint of how the Lord looks at His fallen humanity and grieves over their lost state.

This particular day, I went home and wrote down what I had seen and the impression it had made upon me.

7 April, 1979
A hardness born of despair, a drawn look that gripped me as I sped by. It was come and gone in a moment, but one of a multitude that you see each day.
Yet it has lingered.
You see so many people under pressure these days that I wondered why one more should make such a difference. There was something in the loneliness, the defeat, the fatigue, written into the lines upon the face.
To so many, this was just another number, a statistic, a casualty of life along with thousands of others. What I call the "Queen Street Syndrome". A myriad sea of faces, all nameless, all coming and going but no one knows where.
But is it really so?
I realised that behind that single haunted face in the crowd was a totally unique human being, a soul, a life, a destiny.
Maybe here was a husband, children, a home, a whole world of its own. A world that hadn't been dealt the days very kindly; pressures had driven a future of potential into a sea of despair.
But with so many faces, who has time to care?
I was reminded of where Jesus once spoke of the Good Shepherd leaving the "ninety-and-nine" to go out and find the one that was hurting. I thought of how He took time out for every little child; for the insignificant little woman with the issue of blood, whom He healed. I thought of so many times that He reached out to the lonely and the lost and then I knew...
...there really is Someone that cares. To Him, you're not insignificant, not just a nameless face in a crowd. He knows

your hurt, your sorrow, your trial; and in His love He wants you to know ... He cares!

I felt it so deeply as I wrote it down. But why did it impact me so? Certainly it was for me to pray for the lost and to let me know just how Jesus felt about the people on the streets of our community. But I knew it was more than that and as I prayed and asked God for the answer, it suddenly became so very clear.

Salt is not for itself, it is for the steak! We are called as the light of the world, as salt to be sprinkled. This burden was God's indication to me that He wanted me to be involved. But how? I went again to pray and a bold initiative burst into my mind, *"Take it to the newspaper!"* It seemed impossible. I was a young minister of a small congregation without any real credibility in the secular community. But then God reminded me that the newspaper had printed individual articles about me before, such as the one on the building. It was time to seize the moment.

I headed to the newspaper office and showed them the article and asked if they would print it. To my surprise, they said they would. Emboldened by that positive response, I pressed further. If I was to write one weekly, would they publish it? They said, with a few qualifications, that they would. So I pressed again. Would they be willing to give me my own weekly column called "A Look at Life" with my photograph and the explanation that I was the minister of a local church in the area? After a little discussion and the request that I first write a few for them to see, they again agreed.

It was amazing! Out of one sad face in the crowd had come an incredible opening of influence. "A Look at Life" went on to be a successful weekly column for many years and impacted the lives of thousands of people.

I wonder how many times miracles and significant potentials of breakthrough are never realised because we failed to give credibility to such promptings of the Holy Spirit and act in simple obedience. I wonder how many history-making moments are missed because we fail to trust the Holy Spirit's voice enough and boldly seize the moment.

The other thought that comes to me at this moment is the story of the king who struck the ground with the arrows in 2 Kings 13:18-19. The story goes that the prophet told him to strike the ground with the arrows as a prophetic declaration of how God would strike his enemies for him. He proceeded to strike the ground three times and then stopped. The prophet then told him sadly that the number of times he had struck the ground would now limit the number of victories he would experience. Had he continued to strike the ground, he would have experienced ongoing victories until his enemies were totally shattered.

My excitement at the newspaper printing the first article could have caused me to ignore the Holy Spirit urging me to press them again and again. The outcome would have been a limited victory rather than the ongoing power of influence that God had intended.

Friends, we must not only listen initially but, in proceeding with diligence, continue to listen. We must also cultivate an attitude of perseverance and conquest-mindedness which constantly lives in a state of looking for the greater potential.

Oh, how I know I am speaking directly to some of you right now! Push out the boundaries of your expectations, look for the next horizon, do not settle for that which is more easily obtainable and do not settle for the initial breakthrough. Rather seize the moment, push the advantage, dare to believe that the bigger picture, the grander goal, is possible. It is a matter of obedience and courage.

Not long after "A Look at Life" was launched, I received a telephone call that opened up yet another opportunity to be 'salt' for which I was unprepared for.

"This is Channel One (New Zealand's premier National TV station at that time) and we are wanting to do a series called "The History Makers" on individuals who are making a difference in the nation and are something of a pioneer."

Well, obviously it was a joke! "Oh yeah, and pigs fly backwards around the moon in pink tights!", I replied (or something in that tenor). They must have had that response many a time before as no offence was taken and they proceeded to convince me that this was in fact a very real invitation to be on national television.

A wild flurry of thoughts flooded my mind: "They must have a hidden agenda to sabotage the church"; "Everyone knows you cannot trust the media"; "They will manipulate what you say and you will be misrepresented"; "This is going to expose you and leave you vulnerable"; "They think that I'm a history maker but if they interview me they will find out they have the wrong guy"; "Who put them on to me and told them exaggerated stories to make them interested?"; and "Nothing I am doing is worthy of this and that will quickly become apparent".

And yet, after prayer, I found a strange peace that stilled all the voices and left me with but one which clearly told me to go ahead. I believed that was the Holy Spirit and so agreed to the proposal.

I thought it would be an interview. I was wrong. It was several interviews as well as constant surveillance of me and my family for two weeks, with countless hours of filming by the producer and the crew. They were at the meetings I spoke at, they were in our Sunday services, they dogged our family outings and they even filmed me playing soccer with Margaret and our children. Wherever I was, they were there with their cameras rolling.

When it finally went to air on national television, we were both amazed and grateful that it was, in most part, sincerely edited and portrayed accurately. Only one scene caused negative comments. I had been teaching on parenting and had included (bear in mind this was nearly 30 years ago) a session on disciplining the child.

I had carefully and at length explained the motivation of love and the procedure of explanation and praying with the child, etc., but none of that appeared in the programme. Out of several hours of teaching, they took one story I told in which I had to fill in for the School Principal and apply the rod (as was accepted in those days) to a defiant student who had not submitted voluntarily to receiving the discipline. They had a heyday with that story! In hindsight, I should never have mentioned it with them present but it was then too late. They did not show the outcome of that encounter which was that the young boy reached out to me and we became good friends from that time on.

However, apart from that one incident and the flack that came as a result, the programme was seen as extremely positive and we received an enormous amount of affirmation from around the country. Even that scene was applauded by the great majority who had seen discipline eroding in the schools.

I should stress here that this event was in the 1980's, not the 21st Century. With today's media agenda and bias, one would have to be extremely careful and ensure that legally binding safeguards were in place.

The reason for me including this last story is that in the day and age in which we now live, our lives must be able to stand the scrutiny of a sceptical society. I cannot help but wonder how many Christian leaders today would survive that degree of constant and acute investigation we, as a family, were under for those two weeks. Although we were utterly imperfect and obviously immature, I thank God that our motivation was pure, our finances honest, our morals strong and that we lived with integrity of heart. In fact, this was the comment of the non-Christian TV crew on numerous occasions. It would be true to say that several of them were deeply impacted by the love of God during those two weeks, and not once in that time did we receive anything but positive comment from them personally.

I would encourage you to do an exercise from time to time. Take each and every area of your life and ask the question, "What if this aspect of my life appeared on national TV?" Although that might not happen in this lifetime, we are assured that when we meet Jesus on the day of accountability, it most certainly will. Even the very secrets of hearts will be on the mega screen of Heaven if such events have not been acknowledged and forgiven by His grace. (After which, of course, they cease to exist.)

We have all made some tragic and costly mistakes. There have been times when we haven't handled life well nor responded appropriately. But our Father is the ultimate Redeemer and when we take those events to Him in prayer and humility, they not only are removed from the future Cosmic documentary, but lose their power to afflict us in the present.

What a wonderful thing it will be when Heaven's TV1 is turned on and we can look forward to such an occasion with great anticipation and joy, knowing that we have lived this life to please Him and to bring Him honour.

YOU DID *What?!*

Chapter Twenty

PROPHECY AND PROMISE

It was 1977 and the church was beginning to grow both in numbers and in acceptance. My mind leapt back a full seven years to the days in Takapuna and the scene came vividly into focus.

Margaret and I were married but a short time and both very actively involved in our local church. We were responsible for the Sunday School which we had renamed "Children's Church" due to the changes we had brought. Rather than seeing that ministry as a babysitting exercise with a component of Bible storytelling, we saw it as an awesome opportunity for these children to experience God for themselves and to be involved in ministry. They prayed, they song lead, they preached and they moved in the gifts of the Holy Spirit. It is a tragedy that so many treat our younger members of the Body of Christ as lesser mortals and do not realise the enormous potential that lies within them to become champions of the faith.

Apart from Children's Church, my passion was evangelism. I had been involved in tent evangelism with my previous church, had been a dedicated YWAMmer (Youth with a Mission), and had also been involved in Teen Challenge. To me, the commission was all about getting people saved and discipled for Jesus.

Then along came Sister Kitely. She was a well-respected minister from USA with a very powerful gift of prophecy, and was our guest preacher.

As she ministered in the gift of prophecy to one person after another, I was staggered by her accuracy and obvious flow of the Holy Spirit. Then it was our turn and she directed her comments to me first.

"A teacher shall you be! You shall teach them rows upon rows. Even leaders shall you teach. Yes, a teacher of the Word shall you be!"
What?!!
As she then began to speak to Margaret, my mind went into a flurry of bewilderment and reaction. "Lord, You see that cry in my heart for the heathen. What does she mean with all this stuff about teaching?"

In mid-sentence she stopped speaking to Margaret and whirled around to face me: "Yes! I do see that cry in your heart for the heathen, but you will teach!!"

Unbelievable! I determined not to think another thought whilst that woman was in the room!

After the meeting, I could tell that most of those who knew me as the spontaneous, unstructured, often erratic, explosion of evangelistic fervour that I was, also struggled to see how this woman who had got it so right with everyone else in the room could have so dramatically got it wrong with me. Everyone knew that it would have been easier for God to part the Red Sea than for Him to educate me sufficiently to empower me to teach. And that would be even if I ever had any desire to!

And now here it was, seven years later and the phone was ringing.

It was in the time of charismatic renewal and numbers of more traditional churches were discovering that Jesus was alive and real, and that one could receive the gifts of the Holy Spirit in today's world. It was an exciting time and one in which many reached out for enlightenment and help to understand Scriptures previously blocked from their view.

The request came from a small but beautiful Anglican Church called "St. Peter's on the Hill". They had heard that I was the Pentecostal minister in town and that quite obviously meant I would be an expert on what the Bible said concerning this visitation of the Holy Spirit they were experiencing and what they now should be doing with it.

They had to be kidding! As a young pastor launched into full-time ministry with utterly inadequate training and biblical knowledge, I considered it a miracle that God could keep me one step ahead in preaching to my own congregation. Each Sunday was an exercise in absolute dependence on the Holy Spirit and God's infinite grace and compassion.

Not only did they want me to teach, they wanted me to do it for hours on end, two nights a week! I was panic-stricken. Maybe I could bluff a singular 45 minute talk on the gifts of the Spirit, but an ongoing, systematic exposition of Scripture that was both theologically sound and compelling in delivery sounded like climbing Mt. Everest with my mother-in-law on my shoulders!

And then came Sister Kitely's voice, leaping over that seven years and penetrating my heart like the tip of an arrow: "A teacher shall you be! You shall teach them rows upon rows. Even leaders shall you teach. Yes, a teacher of the Word shall you be!"

I wrestled with God but the word came so strongly to me that I knew He was requiring this step of faith and commitment from me. I said yes.

My world had to change. The discipline of study increased, the thoroughness of investigating experiences in the light of what the Bible teaches had to be thorough. I prayed and read the Word. I pulled out all my Bible School notes from previous years when I had been taught by Rob Wheeler (a great Bible teacher). I brought back to memory all that others had taught on the subject. When finally the night arrived, by God's sheer grace, I was ready.

Night after night, week after week, I taught and was amazed at the anointing of the Holy Spirit to do so. It affected the way I was ministering into my own congregation and many began to comment on the depth of the Word that God was giving me and the teaching series that I brought to the people. Teaching (and, yes, to leaders also) became a major part of my ministry life and has been so to this very day. Most would describe my function as that of a prophet/teacher.

What have I learnt from that? To never judge too quickly the words that God brings to us, regardless of our initial reaction or the vessel through whom God brings it. If you do not understand it, put it on the shelf. God is not in a hurry and will, in His own good timing, bring it back into focus to accomplish that for which He sent it.

I have also learnt that it sometimes takes time, a lot of time. Looking down through the corridors of time through the eyes of divine potential, God could see who and what He was able to make me to be. Just because I could not see the possibility of it, did not deter Him. I am so very grateful that He is neither that fragile nor that fickle to be put off from His intention as long as one's heart is sincere.

Let me say to some of you who feel too many seasons have come and gone since you received your promise: If it was God who spoke it to you, it is alive! Trust Him and place yourself back on the line of unconditional availability and see what our wonderful God of Resurrection and Life can do. It is never too late.

YOU DID *What?!*

Chapter Twenty One

TENDER HEARTS, STEELY RESOLVE

There are divine appointments in life's journey that, when looking back upon them, have proven to be so critical and so vital, that the writing of your own history depended upon their inclusion.

They walked into the church one Sunday morning and sat quietly near the rear, coming not to merely attend a service but to enter into our lives as gifts from God. They were shy and unassuming and could have come and gone almost unnoticed if it were not for the word from God to their hearts.

They had sought God for new direction in their passion to serve Him and follow Him fully, and God had given them a promise: *"I will give to you as a shepherd a man after My own heart."* As they walked into that service those decades ago, God spoke again and told them that they had arrived and I was that one they were to trust. It was a humbling thought then but even more so today as I see what wonderful leaders in the Body of Christ they have become. I speak of Jim and Anneke Shaw.

In today's culture we so often associate true leadership potential with a charismatic personality and forcefulness of expression that is both impressive and obvious. These two were gracious, humble and quiet of spirit. They came not looking for recognition or applause, but to serve and give of themselves for the sake of others. To this very day they have retained that servanthood of spirit even though they successfully lead a local church, have significantly impacted other nations and Jim is on the National Leadership Team in their Movement. Together they stand today as an inspiration to an emerging generation of leaders and their ministry is life-changing to all who know them.

But that was not how it all began.

One occasion, which rather graphically tells you something of those for whom God looks for, was a Sunday service in which I, for some insane and impetuous reason, called out, "Let us have some testimonies!" (Something in those days that you thought you could get away with when you had less than 100 people.) No one moved and silence filled the air as I became more and more embarrassed on the front row. I could feel my toes squirming up inside my shoes.

Jim's only claim to fame that day was where he was sitting. He just happened to be the one sitting behind me as I hissed under my armpit, "Get up and testify!!" Being the ultimate servant that he was (and still is), he walked up behind the pulpit. With a trembling voice he mumbled his way through the first part and then with actual tears, his voice trailed away for those final agonising minutes. I was sweating! And then one of those moments of unrehearsed but absolute agreement took place. I silently screamed out to God, myself and the Cosmos, "He will NEVER get up there again!" Jim simultaneously was doing his own silent screaming, "I will NEVER get up here again!!" On that, we both had absolute and final agreement!

It would be a most dishonouring and unnecessary inclusion in this book if it was not for what happened next.

Some months later, I was praying about whom God would have me appoint as my associate pastor. The congregation was growing and I had one or two men showing an obvious call upon their lives. Jim was not on the list.

Jim was working for the council as a Town Planner and I was looking at a piece of land for future building purposes. He agreed to give me his thoughts on whether or not it would serve our purposes and I picked him up from work.
As we drove some moments down the road I heard this voice say, *"THIS is the pastor for whom you seek!"* What?!! As I swerved violently on the edge of the road, I rebuked this obvious attack upon my sanity.

This led to days of wrestling with God. "Lord, he can't preach!" "God, he is too gracious and shy!" "Father, don't you remember that testimony he gave?" "Father, he is a servant, not a leader." (All of which showed how much I had to learn about true leadership.) God persisted and I initiated the conversation with Jim.

If you think my sense of panic at such a thought was over the top, you should have seen his! I don't know exactly what went through his mind, but reading from his facial expression, it must have been horribly traumatic. There were elements of panic, unbelief and a wrestling with why I would say such a thing to hurt and embarrass him. But was it God? Oh, yes. Jim and his wife, Anneke, soon became my key associates and quite obvious heirs apparent.

As I have seen his leadership over the years and more than once sat in awe at his fluent and powerful delivery of God's Word, I realise that God allowed it to be so back there to teach me firsthand the principle of selection that Samuel discovered when he went those centuries ago to Jesse's home looking for the future king [story account in 1 Samuel 16]. You see, Jim had the one thing that God wanted and considered non-negotiable; a true and honourable heart which loved Him and people unconditionally. His wife, Anneke, possessed that same beautiful simplicity. God knew He could trust these two.

As God looks throughout the world for those who will honour Him, He looks for hearts like Jim and Anneke Shaw. So incredibly tender that weeping came easily when hearing of the pain of another, yet forged with such steel that no demon of Hell nor scheming of man could dent their loyalty to God or to me as their (highly imperfect and human) spiritual leader. For nearly four decades now it has been so. Our love for each other and our mutual esteem grows every year and our bond has stood the multiple tests of ministry pressures, misunderstandings, mistakes, my insecurities, betrayals by others, division in the church and an endless list of events that proved to us again and again what a truly indescribable gift from God they are to not only Margaret and myself, but to their local church, their nation and their world.
(Let me encourage you right here to read my book "An Incorruptible Heart".)

It is tragic that in these decades of seeing God's grace and favour on their lives, I have also seen those with far greater initial giftedness come and go; blown away by winds attracted to their ego and consciousness of their own prowess.

As you will see in the coming chapter, if it were not for their love, support and unswerving loyalty, my own journey could have ended up so very differently.

Any of you reading this who are senior leaders responsible for the development and release of others, please keep this principle ever before your eyes: If God has the heart, He can add all that an individual lacks. But if God does not have their heart, though they are magnificently gifted, they will eventually fall. There is that hidden but persuasive 'Saul' lurking within us all which can only be defeated by a humble and fully surrendered heart.

YOU DID What?!

Chapter Twenty Two

THE RIB GETS VOCAL

In the formative years of our pioneer work in Manurewa, Margaret was involved in leading the ladies' work and assisting me in counselling and decision making. She was vitally involved in every aspect of our ministry but had our marriage and our three children as her primary responsibility in those years. Consequently, she did not get involved in platform preaching and teaching at that time.

However, as time passed and the children grew, that began to change.

Our own marriage had known challenges and considerable difficulties which had resulted in our seeking God for answers. Margaret was passionate about us having a marriage that really honoured the Lord and was a good example to our children and those who knew us. It was her passion and diligence which led us to discovering so much that enlightened and strengthened our relationship.

We lived in an era with few resources on the subject of marriage and family. Families were in vital need and God stirred us to try and help.

Margaret's quest to read and study all she could find on marriage and family soon began to show itself in her wisdom and instruction to others. She then began to write a book for married women that led me to doing one for the men. Eventually she overcame her apprehension at public speaking and joined me in speaking at marriage seminars.

Very soon, Margaret was receiving invitations to speak at ladies' groups and then conferences. I remember on two occasions large conferences in Australia flew her over the Tasman to be the primary speaker. Everywhere she spoke there were incredible responses as women heard her share principles of hope, wisdom and life.

Her example goaded me to commence a seminar for men called "The Husband's Role", which went on to become wonderfully used of the Lord to bring enlightenment to a generation of men who were still largely chauvinistic without realising it.

Some years ago, Margaret headed up a parenting course at CityLife Church called "Growing Families God's Way", which is outstanding material written by Gary and Ann-Marie Ezzo. She went on to introduce that material into several churches with wonderful fruit evidenced in the emerging generation.

It has been our joy to minister together over the years on these subjects and we still do so today. The tragedy is that even though it is more desperately needed today, it is less of a priority in the minds of people. With marriage disasters and divorces on the increase and the strain of that obvious in the church, there is less hunger and commitment to find godly solutions. A seminar on marriage will have vastly less numbers than one on the prophetic. This is an imbalance which needs to be addressed if the Church of the 21st century is to emerge strong and healthy.

When I consider the beauty of our marriage today and the love of our family, I am so very grateful for Margaret's passion, diligence and perseverance in those earlier years. Not only did she play the major role for good in our own family, but was the one who researched, prepared and inspired the material we shared with so many others.

Although Margaret continues to speak as opportunities present themselves, her main priority is to selflessly pour her life into our extended family, my own ministry and those of the team. Her instinctive motherhood extends to everyone on our DMM team and her wisdom, encouragement and sense of sheer fun are truly the glue that holds us all together.

Friends, let me challenge you with this thought. Other than your personal intimacy with the Lord, there is no greater priority (if you are married!) than your spouse and then your children. I urge you to reflect that priority in your time and focus, and make that quest for excellence a thing of great joy together.

YOU DID What?!

Chapter Twenty Three

BREATHING AIR ON EVEREST

They say those who climb Mt. Everest find one of their greatest challenges is the thinness of the air up there. It has a way of distorting reality and making it hard to breathe. Without proper training and a supply of oxygen, even the most skilled climber will come to grief.

With Jim and the rest of the leadership team in place, the church had a season of substantial growth and we saw the numbers go from about 80 people up to nearly 400, and this in a time well before the mega church.

With faith and enthusiasm running high, we built a new Christian school and bought a prime piece of land to build again. A site of 13 acres was chosen, right alongside the freeway and close to the off ramp, with a house already on it for a manse. I remember well the day that Winkie Pratney and Barry McGuire stood on that huge concrete slab with the comment, "There is no tunnel vision here!" We hit the newspapers with our design which had the largest singular span wooden beam ever to be placed within a building of our kind.

By this stage the Movement had asked me to go on to the National Leadership Team, and I had become well accepted nationally and internationally as a prophet.

Popularity was high and I discovered that 'everyone loves a winner'. Invitations to preach. Invitations to dinner. Invitations to be involved. The smell of success was like that air on Everest.

But let me tell you that you do not discover your true friends in a time of peace but in a time of war. It is only in times of controversy that the true hearts of men and women are revealed. This was soon to become apparent.

I have purposely made this my shortest chapter because, as I view my life and God's purposes in it, the period of enjoying that rarefied air has had the least to teach me. In its intoxication, it can make you lose your acute sense of dependence and desperate cry to hear His voice in all matters of choice and decision. One simply becomes confident in one's general state of spirituality and begins to feel that God will bless whatever you set your hand to do.

It was not that I had any conscious thought of spending less time in prayer or study of the Word and my love for the Lord was still burning bright, but that deep inner cry of desperately needing God to speak on every issue of significance lost its focus and intensity. In such an euphoric state, one begins to enjoy the ride like a hang glider soaring above the masses, forgetting who it is that controls those airwaves.

In the hidden motives of men's hearts, those airwaves were changing and a storm was gathering.

Chapter Twenty Four

THE DARK NIGHT OF THE SOUL

I t is said that God is incredibly thorough in all matters of His creation. As He prepares us for what is to be His ultimate calling on our lives, He is no less thorough. In matters of faith and enlargement of spirit, this can be both challenging and exhilarating at the same time. Much like being hurled off the top of a mountain on a hang glider without any training, and having the assurance that He will control the air currents.

In matters of wisdom, principle, character and preparedness to identify with the wounds of others, it is more like having the hang glider disintegrate in midair and finding oneself bouncing off the rocks at

YOU DID What?!

the bottom of the ravine!

My years of flying high and above were about to experience a sudden downdraft and the rocks were mercilessly real. The 'big one' struck for Margaret and I, and we found ourselves in our 'dark night of the soul'. It was a very rapid descent from what had been considered a great success to absolute disaster; a stripping of finances, prestige, building, Christian school, our home, and of course, friends.

My errors were not those of some great moral fall, but errors of judgement. Decisions concerning leadership, decisions concerning the size of the building project, decisions concerning the amount of travel and ministry I was involved in at the time, which distanced me from my leaders and the congregation at a time when they needed the personal touch the most.

It was not a case of intentionally doing wrong but one of making unwise judgements.

The whole glorious, furious pace of achievement had clouded my need to hear intimately from the King in matters of detail. Oh, the vision may have been His, but as I now understand, the execution must also be His.

The consequences were swift in becoming apparent.

An offshore contract we had signed with a bank turned out to be a disaster. We had signed over omnipotent powers to a small group of Foreign Exchange Advisors who proceeded to 'buy and sell' on the international market using our money!

It was a nightmare. In a matter of months they took a $650,000 loan and produced a debt of over $1,000,000! (And that was in the 80s!) Every day the phone would ring with more and more bad news. I had our lawyer working to get us out of the contract but it was deemed impossible without paying back the original loan in its entirety. This we could not do as we had, of course, spent that money on the building project.

People started coming to the door wanting answers. Answers I did not have.

We finally began making those painful decisions which had become unavoidable. We had never failed to make a payment by its due date and we agreed that it would be dishonouring to the Lord to allow commitments to go unpaid. There was no alternative. We sold the property. With the sale of the property, came the sale of the building so many had laboured on for so many long months with sacrificial toil.

Our Christian school that had taken five years to build up also had to be closed. The parents were faced with the decision of what to do with the education of their children. This was so very difficult for me and many others. Oh, how we loved that school and all those vibrant, wonderful kids.

Two homes on the property, one of them the house our own family was living in, also had to go. People were confused and bewildered, and a number of them, understandably, simply left for less complicated waters.

How my heart ached for them. The pain I felt was not just for Margaret and me but it was for them as well. Precious, beautiful people that I loved but now seemed so unable to protect from this awful reality.

As things deteriorated, it was necessary to stand before the congregation and ask their forgiveness for the hurt caused to so many. I went to the church that day dazed at how all this could be happening.

Then the gossip started. We learned afresh the power of discouraging and accusing words. Some of those we had loved the most, were those who wounded the deepest.

Some got 'revelations' on how this was a God-given judgement to purge the land from 'false prophets'.

In the midst of this non-relenting barrage of discouragement, one of those on my leadership team shared that he felt to start up his own church just down the road in a nearby suburb. I was shattered! This man was my friend, not just any member of my team. I had looked to him for support and encouragement. How could this be happening?

It became apparent that not only was this going to happen, but that a large number of the people and some of the leadership had been persuaded to join him in the endeavour. After all, my own leadership appeared to be in tatters and an alternative at that time must have seemed incredibly appealing. My requests to postpone this process and to reconsider it after we were out of the crisis were not successful.

It is not for me to judge their heart in this matter as they sincerely felt that what they were doing was right, but it did not stop me feeling stunned and deeply wounded. I realised that this had enormous potential to bring contention should we declare our opposition to it and polarise people into taking sides on the issue. As the key person concerned could not be persuaded to reconsider, the only alternative was to publicly 'bless' the new initiative and release people who wanted to go.

The weeping was done in private but at the pulpit, I made it clear that there should be no negativity about this and that we wished them well. In my emotionally and spiritually depleted state, it was one of the hardest things I have ever had to do.

Our 'dark night of the soul' had arrived. Margaret and I discovered in new depth the dealings of the Lord. We had to wrestle with forgiving those involved. We wept together and apart. Our life was becoming rubble and we cried out in our bewilderment.

In the midst of it, we had many choices. But one choice stood out above all others - would we respond God-ward or react man-ward? Would we see the hand of God's allowance and run to the cross, or would we fight for our 'rights'?

I thank God today that we clung to the cross. Daily His grace became our sufficiency.

I realised that the "He owes us nothing" statement was in fact a great and awesome truth. He has already given us everything in the person of His Son. If stripped naked but still accepted by His grace, we are immeasurably wealthy.

After the smoke had cleared and we had relocated, one part of the church remaining with us in Manurewa and the other part going to the nearby suburb, Margaret and I took the children to Seattle, USA for two months to get counsel from godly people and to pour our souls out before the Lord. We had so many questions, so many hurtful memories and so many aching voids because of friendships ripped out of our lives. It took all the time we had allotted. But oh, how He met us!

He stripped us, He broke us, He exposed those inner realities never faced before. It was so thorough, until finally nothing seemed left but our love for Him. Forgiveness and genuine love filled our hearts toward those who we felt had wounded us. We came to see that the vast majority of those who had gone to commence the new church were good, godly people responding to what appeared to be the reality of that time.

Then came the rebuilding, the resurrection, the fresh commissioning. What a gracious God we serve! How easy it is now to pour out our praise and adoration.

And it is in such times that we learn and discover keys of life for the benefit of others. As we now look back upon that season, we do not do so with hurt but with gratitude as we see the immeasurable wealth God put inside of us at that time. Now, when ministering to pastors and leaders all over the world, we draw more principles out of that 'dark night of the soul' than from any other chapter of our lives.

Father had allowed it, Father had redeemed it, and Father had turned it into a well of life.

In the midst of all of this, God graciously gave us those who stood firm and loyal. Theirs was a testimony of resilience and unshakeable faith. Their motives and faithfulness had been sorely tested but not found wanting. They became lifelines in the midst of a sea of whirlpools drawing us downwards into a depth of despair.

There are too many to mention, but they are all equally precious to us today and bonded to us for life. Jim and Anneke shone brightest in that darkest of hours, along with the most wonderful friend and intercessor, Jacky Stevens (now Jacky Squires). There are so many others and you know who you are. God most certainly does and the rewards laid up for each of you will declare most loudly that God saw every tear and moment of moral strength. My gratitude to each of you is as great now as it was then. Thank you.

What a season like that demonstrates is that if we keep our hearts free from negative and destructive emotions, God will ultimately redeem even our weaknesses and errors of judgement. Keeping a spirit of humility and maintaining a selfless love for God and His people allows God to re-fashion the broken vessels and restore them again to a place of honour.

Perhaps the key principle God spoke to me during that time was:

"Keep your intimacy with God and your integrity with people."

If we accomplish these two things, our Father will undoubtedly write the next chapter.

YOU DID What?!

Chapter Twenty Five

LEARNING TO DIE

I have told you in brief concerning the experience we had in Seattle but I need to share with you, in much more detail, one of the most critical experiences of my ministry life.

Before leaving Manurewa, I had shared with Jim concerning the nature of what I saw lying ahead. That year had been filled with such tragedy and disappointment, and I had come to the conclusion that God no longer wanted me to be the senior pastor of that local church. Amazingly, invitations were still coming in for me to minister as a prophet to the Body of Christ, and I believed that God would have me transition to the life of a full-time itinerant prophet.

Although I was going to Seattle to seek the face of the Lord and to hear His voice, in my own heart I had made up my mind and I shared with Jim the way I saw it happening in the future. In essence, I gave him the local church and shared with him that he more than deserved it. We were both aware of the number of times people had prophesied over him that he would be a senior leader and a significant leader in the Body of Christ. In addition, by this stage, I knew it to be the dream of his heart. This then was the basis upon which we left to go to Seattle.

The first few weeks were taken up with us weeping profusely into the carpet and crying out to God. Finally, the day of breakthrough came and I began to feel His presence filling the room. With great anticipation, I listened to hear His confirmation of my intended journey ahead. After an overwhelming sense of His love for me, I did indeed begin to hear His voice clearly but what He said took me completely by surprise.

"Die to the prophetic! That local church is your responsibility, and I desire that you go back and pick up that responsibility again, and bring it back into a place of honour and health."

I was shocked! For three long days, I wrestled with what God had said to me.

Finally, I came to the conclusion that if I was ever going to be happy, it would only be doing that which I knew He wanted me to do. I took my 'Isaac' and placed him upon the altar and put the knife in my hand. I wrote letters to all those who had shown interest in me coming to minister as a prophet and shared with them that I was no longer available for such ministry now or in the future. The manner in which God had spoken to me the phrase *"die to the prophetic"* had not communicated any sense of this being merely for a season.

It was God's grace which had brought me to such a place of obedience, but now I was faced with another dilemma. Unofficially, I had in essence given the local church to Jim, and he was now running ahead with it. The anointing of God had come upon him and the response from the people had been wonderful. By all concerned, it was now assumed that Jim was the new senior leader of that local church. If I was to now try and take that position back to myself, I could see nothing but heartache and contention being the result.

The majority were already accepting Jim as the senior leader, and Jim himself would be disappointed and rightfully so. After all he had been through in the previous crisis, this would be the final blow and I could see that our friendship would be the casualty.

But knowing that God had spoken to me so clearly, I had no option. I reached for the phone and rang Jim to share the news with him. His response at that moment is something I have shared in leadership conferences around the world: "David, I have never sought to complicate our relationship. Whatever God asks you to do, that is what I will do with all my heart!" I was overwhelmed with gratitude - gratitude for God's intervention and grace, and gratitude for Jim's Christlike spirit and servant heart.

From that very moment, Jim began to prepare the way for our return. He selflessly laid aside his own desires and dreams of being the senior leader and worked to freshly inspire the people in my own leadership and the future with me as the senior leader. A few weeks later, Margaret and I returned home to a standing ovation and an avalanche of love and affection!

I had died to the dream of being a prophet to the nations, and Jim had died to his dream of being the senior leader of that local church. A few days after my return, Jim came into my office and said that he would be honoured to serve me as my number two for the rest of his life. To this day, I cannot think of that moment without emotion. It still stands out as one of the most powerful demonstrations of true humility and love for God that I have ever seen expressed.

As Jim and I worked with the rest of the team and as God's favour flowed, we saw the restoration of that body of people and also of the finances. God's response had been abundant and the church began to steadily grow again.

A few months later, I was sitting in my office when the phone rang. It was a well-known apostolic leader in our nation who informed me that he and two or three others had been in prayer the previous day and had the word of the Lord for me. It was time, they said, for me to be released from the local church to serve the Body of Christ in an apostolic and prophetic role. It was time, they said, for me to hand the reins over to Jim and for him to be officially set in as the new senior leader of that local church. I told them I had heard too clearly from God about that subject to even listen to their suggestion!

The following day the phone rang again, and this time it was a leading prophet in Australia who gave me the identical message! The next day I attended the local ministers' fraternal and was met at the door by two ministers, from different denominations, who I deeply respected. They then proceeded to tell me how God had urged them to get together to pray and that the result of their praying was that they had a message to deliver to me. Again, it was identical!

Over the period of four days, five different sets of senior brethren in the Body of Christ rang me to give me that same message. Margaret and I shared it with Jim and his wife Anneke, and after much prayer, we came to the conclusion that God had indeed spoken to us.

On March 6th 1988, national leaders from several different denominations came together at our local church and released Margaret and myself to the itinerant life and placed Jim and Anneke in as the new senior leaders of that local church. It was just 9 months after we returned from Seattle.

Friends, if we are not willing to die, we do not qualify to live. It is a principle we see again and again in Scripture that out of the death of self and its desires (often most legitimate) comes forth life. Sometimes it takes greater faith and obedience to lay something down than it does to pick it up.

A new era had begun!

Chapter Twenty Six

NO SALARY WITH ABUNDANCE

With the coming of itinerant life, there came a whole new set of challenges. The transition from a predictable salary to living by faith demands a whole new level of trust. It requires a retraining of the mind to be dependent upon God's faithfulness rather than how much your salary package will allow.

As God knows the reluctance of our humanity to give up its own sense of control, He is often left with no option but to arrange circumstances which leave us without a choice.

YOU DID What?!

We had earlier accepted the generous offer of the church Trust to lend us the deposit for a home (we had previously sold our home to put the equity into the building fund). The arrangement was that we would revalue our home two years later and return the money plus a share of the increased equity. It was an excellent arrangement for both the Trust and us, as house values were steadily and 'predictably' rising.

However, not long after, the unthinkable happened and house prices began to fall, and fall, and fall, and fall!!! By the time we had to start thinking about a repayment to the Trust, all equity in the house was gone and values were still falling. We had gone into it with all good intentions and integrity of heart, but what now?

We were self-supporting itinerants, living very much month to month with nothing to spare, and our home was now worth no more than our mortgage!

The Trust was wonderful and told us "not to worry" and that "none of us could have seen this thing coming". But the laws of the Kingdom clearly state that one must honour one's contracts (owe no man anything).

We were in need of a giant miracle! A $30,000 miracle! And that was in 1988!

To a self-supporting itinerant believing on a month to month basis, it may as well have been $30 million! Praying got started in earnest. "Jehovah Jireh!" became a daily declaration.

Then there came the invitation - a cry for help from churches in the USA. They needed me over there for an extended period of about three months and they would pay my fare, etc.

But we had a major problem. Margaret and I had very firmly nailed into place our value system and that value system included the family coming before the ministry. I certainly could not be separated from them for so long and still honour that commitment. In times like that you discover whether you have a convenient persuasion or a genuine heart conviction.

I came to the conclusion it would cost at least $10,000 to take the whole family with me for that period of time (over and above the expected honorariums, etc.). It was obviously impossible. I simply could not go.

I explained to the Lord that I was already crying out to Him for the 'parting of the Red Sea' with the $30,000, and it would be ridiculous for me to even consider the trip. I was sure He would agree.

But I was wrong. The drawing to go continued to increase and every day became a wrestling with the situation.

Three or four days into this process, Margaret came in and showed me a prophecy given to us about a year before, from a visiting prophet to New Zealand who had no idea who we were. It was an amazingly accurate word in every detail and had within it the situation we were facing exactly. It said that at the time when these events would unfold, we were to believe the Lord, commit ourselves to go beyond the point of no return, and we would be amazed at what the Lord would do.

It was too accurate and too detailed, and there was the leaping of the Holy Spirit in our hearts. It was illogical and totally unreasonable, but we both had a deep conviction that this was all orchestrated by the Lord to somehow show the power of His own miraculous supply. We said yes and made all arrangements to go, including the booking of the tickets.

Now I was beseeching Jehovah Jireh for $40,000!!!

YOU DID What?!

Here's where it all gets rather exciting. And this is what happened.

A group of businessmen in Auckland City (anonymous to this very day) had apparently met to pray together. The Lord spoke to them and said, *"I want you to give some money away."* They said, "But Lord, who to?" He replied, *"David McCracken."* They went to their pastor to check it out and he told them he witnessed that this was of God and that they should go back and ask how much. They did and the Lord gave them a clear answer. They channelled the money via that pastor's local church in order to remain anonymous. The pastor then rang and arranged to visit us.

He said we had better sit down before he commenced, and then told us the story and handed us the cheque. It was for $50,000!!!

I am not often speechless but that one left me gasping for air! It was like a testimony you read about in a 'miracle' magazine. That sort of a thing doesn't happen to 'ordinary people'. Well, this time it did.

We were completely overwhelmed and in tears.

We paid back the Trust and went on the trip, which turned out to be one of the highlights of our ministry and family lives. In every way it was successful and totally God-ordained.

What a totally awesome God we really serve! For Him nothing is impossible if we are endeavouring to walk in obedience to His will and purpose.

I have often said that we all would love to 'walk on water' but that is not really the question. The question is, "How many want to get out of the boat?!" You see, even we Irish can figure out the basics. You can't walk on the water while you are still in the boat!

Everybody wants the miraculous testimony. Everybody wants to be able to say how God sovereignly intervened and supplied them miraculously with 'the manna and the quails', but not too many want to be in the circumstances where such a miracle is actually necessary.

Most of the time, if we can handle it ourselves, the Lord will let us. He doesn't part the Red Sea just to demonstrate His muscles. But when we know that it is impossible in our own strength and supply, and we desperately need Him or we sink; when we cry out in total dependence upon Him and in all integrity of heart believe ourselves to be in the centre of His will and purpose; well, that's different.

Endurance is necessary.

There is an interesting passage in 1 Samuel 14 where Jonathan and his armour-bearer are taking on thousands of well-armed Philistines. It was just the two of them against an army of well-trained veterans of war.

Read the following verses and then I will comment.

1 Samuel 14:12-15, 19-20, 23
12 *Then the men of the garrison called to Jonathan and his armour-bearer, and said, "Come up to us, and we will show you something." Jonathan said to his armour-bearer, "Come up after me, for the LORD has delivered them into the hand of Israel."*
13 *And Jonathan climbed up on his hands and knees with his armour-bearer after him; and they fell before Jonathan. And as he came after him, his armour-bearer killed them.*
14 *That first slaughter which Jonathan and his armour-bearer made was about twenty men within about half an acre of land.*
15 *And there was trembling in the camp, in the field, and among all the people. The garrison and the raiders also trembled; and the earth quaked, so that it was a very great trembling...*
19 *Now it happened, while Saul talked to the priest, that the noise which was in the camp of the Philistines continued to increase; so Saul*

said to the priest, "Withdraw your hand."
20 *Then Saul and all the people who were with him assembled, and they went into battle; ...*
23 *So the LORD saved Israel that day, and the battle shifted to Beth Aven.*

Note verse 14:
Jonathan and his armour-bearer were not fighting children but well-armed, well-trained men of war. To have fought and killed twenty of them over half an acre of land would have taken a considerable amount of time. Where do you think the rest of the Philistines were during this time that Jonathan was despatching their brethren? Standing at a distance watching? No! They were, by this time, fully surrounding them.

Why is this so important? Because Jonathan and his armour-bearer were now beyond the point of no retreat! And only then did God get in on the act!

As Jonathan and his armour-bearer came out of their tents that morning, there was no earthquake. As they marched across the valley floor, the heavens were silent. As they scaled up the side of that hill to meet the enemy, God didn't say a word. As they pulled their swords from their sheaths and struck the first blow, there was still no supernatural intervention. There was a notable silence and a lack of God's apparent presence.

But when Jonathan and his armour-bearer got beyond the point of no return, then God shook the earth! When their commitment was total and the possibility of negotiation was removed, God intervened in the most miraculous of ways.

Hebrews 10:36 tells us that *we have need of endurance, so that after we have done the will of God, we may receive the promise.*

Today we live in an instant society in which we press buttons and gain results. Perseverance and endurance are woefully absent in the bulk of our generation who live in our Western culture. And yet such character attributes are going to be vitally necessary if we are to more accurately represent Jesus Christ in the turbulent days ahead.

The King of the Church knows this only too well and consequently allows circumstances in our lives that will demand of us a developing of these attributes. One must wonder how many times it is that saints have come to within an inch of their miracle only to lose it by quitting their prayer and intercession a day early.

YOU DID What?!

Chapter Twenty Seven

BURNOUT AND PROVISION

You would have thought after an experience of the magnitude described in the previous chapter that my sense of dependence upon the Lord's supply would have been complete. But not so.

My faith in God for a one-off miracle had certainly been increased, but in my mind, I associated that with a specific commission to go to the States at that time. His supply for predictable groceries and rent was another thing entirely.

Back then there was a well-known phrase amongst itinerant min-

YOU DID What?!

isters: "Meetings equals eatings". That, coupled with a sense of the need to prove my diligence to God, drew me more and more into a lifestyle of compulsive preaching engagements. This was immediately after 15 years of virtually nonstop ministry in the local church and 3 years of intense spiritual and emotional challenges as described earlier.

After my first year of itinerant life, in which I preached in a ridiculous number of meetings, I was struck with coronary artery disease and burnout. I was only 40 years old and my whole world began to collapse around me. My mind was filled with a myriad of questions as to why God had allowed this as I was so faithfully serving Him. I had not yet fully discovered Him as the Master Potter of my life, and the One who was the ultimate Redeemer of all circumstances. He was, in fact, orchestrating one of the most exciting and instructive seasons of my life, but at that time I couldn't see it.

The first lesson came one morning when I was sitting in a chair feeling most despondent. A car drove up our driveway and I glanced out the window to see who could be visiting us, hoping it was one of my close friends who would encourage me. But instead I saw someone I had not expected to see at that time.

Brent Douglas was a minister who was known for his love for those who were struggling; he cared enough to get involved, not just talk about it. He had helped several in their time of need and was also pioneering a good church in Auckland.

However, I had always considered him a little loud and brash. With my over-sensitive nature and substantial insecurities, I found his bold directness of speech rather overwhelming at times. There were even moments when I found myself judging his boldness and thinking he should wear a muzzle! I now know of course that it was simply a difference in our callings and in our dispositions. But at that time, in my vulnerable emotional state, he represented a potential tsunami!

I braced myself as he walked into the room.

After a few moments of polite chitchat, he then reached into his pocket and drew out an envelope and placed it upon the table. He said, "David, we love you, and we desire to see you restored and back into ministry. This will be sent to you each month for as long as it takes." Inside that envelope was $500! And that was still in those 80s I keep mentioning! He also brought a box of groceries and offered to take me fishing in his boat when I felt I was ready for it.

He then went on to say that anything he could do to help, I'd only have to ask for. I was overwhelmed with gratitude.

Friends, perhaps God has His miracle answer for you but it is coming through a vessel you would least expect. When we have judgemental attitudes toward our brethren, God will ultimately find ways to confront those attitudes. At times, it will involve Him using the subject of your judgement as the means for your miracle.

Since then, Brent and I have had decades of friendship and mutual appreciation.

$500 a month was a lot of money in those days, but still well less than what was needed to pay the mortgage and support a wife and three growing children. We were still in a position of great dependence and that is exactly where God wanted us to be.

I remember the story of a man who climbed a cliff by the sea. It was well over 100 metres high, and nothing below but jagged rocks and certain death. As he neared the top of the cliff, he suddenly found himself with nowhere to place his hands and feet and began to slide backwards. Realising his peril, he screamed out for help, "Is there anyone up there?!" *"Yes!"*, boomed the reply. "Who are you?" ... *"God!"* ... "Can you help me?"... *"Yes!"* ... "What do you want me to do?" ... *"Let go of the branch!"* ... "Is there anyone else up there?!!"

YOU DID *What?!*

Friends, it is scary to <u>totally trust God for your provision.</u> Yet it is a place we all must come to. God, knowing this, will at times orchestrate events which leave us with no option, and it is His unrelenting love for us which causes it to be so. He knows it is only in the place of total dependence and trust that we will find our ultimate freedom from the tyranny of being ruled by the dollars in the bank.

As our last little bit of reserve ran out, our prayer intensified. And that's when it all began.

Money started to arrive in the mail from people we hardly knew and some we didn't know at all. Week by week, day by day, His sufficiency continued to flow as and when it was needed.

On one occasion, a pastor from Singapore for whom we had ministered only once a few years back, came to visit. He said how God had spoken to him and some friends at a leadership meeting to take up a love offering for us. He then proceeded to pour this bag full of Singaporean money onto our kitchen table! It was all we needed and more.

After several months of this incredible supply, I remember the day I sat back in my chair and said, "Lord, this is incredible!" *"But have you got the point?!"* was His reply. I said, "Yes, Lord. I do not depend on meetings for my supply nor will I depend upon man. I depend entirely upon You as my Great Provider".

It was then He spoke a phrase that had me riveted: *"Aren't you glad you did not consume the seed?"* Over the next few minutes as He spoke clearly to my heart, I saw a principle which has been a critical part of our walking in financial freedom.

When we had received our miracle provision of $50,000, our actual need was only $40,000. I figured at the time that $5,000 was our tithe to the local church and the other $5,000 was to upgrade our well-worn car. But it was at that moment the Holy Spirit spoke, *"Don't you dare consume the seed!"* I had never heard the phrase before.

He then quickened to me 2 Corinthians 9:10 where it tells us that every time God provides for us, there is both seed for the sower and bread for the eater. He then went on to tell me that as I had petitioned Him for $40,000, that's what I should have been happy with when it arrived. He had not been confused as to my request, and therefore had a specific purpose in the supply of the extra $5,000. He then directed Margaret and I to give that $5,000 away to a needy family.

The extra $5,000 had simply been a seed given to us for the time of need that was coming. I have no doubt at all that if we had consumed that $5,000 in our time of surplus, we would not have had the miracle supply during my time of illness. In His foreknowledge, God had simply supplied the necessary seed for the challenge He knew lay ahead. He was working to a universal law which He Himself had established.

I believe the reason why so many people today do not see answers to their prayers for provision, is that on a previous occasion when they received abundance, they did not ask God where to sow the seed.

After 10 months, I was finally ready to resume the life of an itinerant.

Looking back now, I am filled with a sense of gratitude for that apparent time of physical contradiction. Over the years I have seen so many itinerants struggle with finances, often leaving their calling for no other reason than that they have not been able to embrace the life of total dependence. I have seen pastors and leaders struggle with believing God for the supernatural miracle element of God's supply. I thank God for those ten months which brought Margaret and me into the financial freedom we now enjoy.

It seems such a simple thing to say, but God really does know what He is doing when He fashions us and moulds us. He knows that at times this must involve bringing us to a place where we have no option but to surrender humanity's control and place ourselves unconditionally in His hands.

Chapter Twenty Eight

EMBRACING KANGAROOS

For the first five years of itinerant life, we remained as part of the local church in Manurewa. On occasions I would receive an invitation to minister in Australia and I would enjoy those times, but always found it to be a harsh land compared with the gentle nature of New Zealand. At times I speculated that it may have had something to do with the fact that Australia was founded by convicts and New Zealand was founded by missionaries! It was a great place to visit and a great place to come home from.

Let me insert here, for those Aussies who would now like to use my book to light their next barbecue, that I am now an Australian citizen and loving every minute of it! For two decades now I have walked with kangaroos (bush walk near my house), swatted flies, grown to love the green and gold, and completely fallen in love with OUR nation. So stick with the story and see how it turns out.

On one of those visits, I was preaching on the stage of what was then known as Waverley Christian Fellowship (now CityLife Church) in Melbourne, and I remember they had flags from all the different nations around the wall of the auditorium. As I glanced up from the platform, I noticed there was a space that had no flag on it and the Holy Spirit whispered into my heart, *"There is a place here for you!"* That brief whisper began a process of God speaking to me about shifting our family to live in Australia.

That may not sound like such a big deal to you but let me put it into context. For years I had watched various ministers leave New Zealand for either Australia or USA and, when questioned about this possibility for myself, I loudly declared that I would never do so. I had one standard reply: "Never!" My friends, be very careful about declaring that which you will never do.

Adding to the embarrassment of my long-standing confession, there was the issue of my credibility. Although I had had several visits to Australia for ministry, I was relatively unknown and the opportunities to minister would be very limited. It would be like starting from scratch all over again.

And then there was the house. We had bought the house in a time of high prices, but were now experiencing a deep slump. The value of our home was barely above what we owed on our mortgage. The decision to sell at that time would look like financial disaster.

But the Lord continued to speak clearly to my heart and so I shared it with Margaret. I will never forget her reply: "Our children have been birthed here, all the relatives live here, their grandparents live here, our friends are all here. Read my lips! We…are…not…going!!" One look at her countenance told me the futility of arguing and I told God it was His problem. He knew I had made a covenant to never take a step of obedience or faith without Margaret's approval. A covenant which may sound irresponsible to you, but believe me, it is one which has saved my bacon a dozen times.

God knows my disposition, and my default response is always one of "Let's do it now!" so He gave me a partner He could use, when necessary, to restrain my impetuosity. I have lost count of the number of times I would have ended up in disaster if it had not been for the wisdom of Margaret's counsel. Not because I had not heard the right direction to take, but because I had not waited to receive the finer detail of the timing. It is a tragedy that many strong visionary leaders do not listen to the one God has given to them to prevent such disasters.

When God's timing did eventually arrive, He used a prophet in Australia (whose local church we were visiting) to clearly speak to Margaret's heart without any of my involvement whatsoever. From the moment she heard God speak clearly to her, she set her resolve to fully obey that which God was asking of us.

It has never been an issue of obedience with Margaret. However, in order to obey boldly, she must know in her heart of hearts that it is God speaking. Neither has it been an issue of submission, but one of honouring the covenant we had made together to work as a team. She knows that if she does not speak that which is truly in her heart, she will dishonour the covenant we had made. If I was to come back to her, after appropriate prayer and seeking God, and still be firmly of that persuasion, I have no doubt she would loyally support the decision I had to make as the spiritual head of our home. It has just never been an issue.

On the flight back to Auckland from Melbourne, we realised we had one major challenge still ahead. Our children (then aged 21, 19 and 17) had only ever known the environment of that one local church, and it was true that their grandparents, relatives and friends all lived in New Zealand. We simply did not know how we could possibly tell them that they had to now leave it all behind. Oh, how we underestimated God's grace in that situation.

As we entered the arrival hall at the airport, our children were there to greet us. Steve looked us in the eyes and simply asked the question, "Well, when are we moving to Australia?"
"What! How could you possibly know?"
"Really, Dad! Don't you believe that we can also hear from God?!"

And so the decision was made. We sold all that we had, said goodbye to relatives and friends, and winged our way to a whole new beginning in life.

Chapter Twenty Nine

A SHOCK, A LAKE AND AN IRISH JIG

Margaret and I were 45 years old when we landed in Australia to begin our new venture of faith. And yet we felt in our hearts very much like the 25 year olds who had set out to pioneer 20 years before.

We had a teenage family, a very small amount of money, very few ministry invitations, and no sense of knowing which church we were to settle in. Our close friends, Kevin and Dariel Forlong, were the senior ministers of the church known as Westside AOG at that time, and welcomed us with open arms during our time of discovering the will of God. They helped find us a home to rent, they embraced us, introduced us to people, and were our constant support in those early months. Although we did not end up remaining in that local church, we remain very close friends and Kevin is now on our Board and I am on his.

It was then I remembered what happened while preaching on the platform of Waverley Christian Fellowship two years earlier. I remembered those words "There is a place here for you", and also recalled the number of times the senior minister, Kevin Conner, had visited New Zealand, and our appreciation of him as a father figure in the Gospel. As strange as it may sound, it had not been a decision in my heart at that point, but we collectively as a family decided that it was worth a visit.

Without making any enquiries, we got in the car and drove over to the far side of the city and walked in the door. We found ourselves in the midst of a service already underway and filled with youth. It was their young people's service, but we decided to stay anyway. Margaret and I seated ourselves in the back row while our three children sought out seats closer to the front.

As the passionate singing gathered us up into worship, we immediately felt a sense of God confirming that we had found a place in which to put down our roots. If we needed any further confirmation, we got it some moments later at the 'meet and greet' time as our three children came up to us excitedly and said, "Stop looking! This is going to be our spiritual home!"

It was very hard telling Kevin and Dariel as we had all assumed we would make our spiritual home with them. However, Father could see the future and we could not. He knew that Kevin and Dariel would not be remaining as the senior ministers of that local church, and today they are successful itinerant ministers, carrying a powerful message to the Body of Christ.

We found a new place to rent, and by this time had bought an older Mitsubishi Magna car, but felt in our hearts that God wanted to give us our own home again. Because we had sold our home in the slump, we had come to Australia with insufficient funds to go towards a normal deposit. Once again, we found ourselves in need of a miracle intervention.

One Monday, as I returned from an interstate ministry trip, Margaret met me at the airport and as we drove home, she calmly told me that on the Saturday, she had gone out and bought us a block of land! I couldn't believe my ears! She waited for me to regain myself from my state of shock (and extreme verbal panic) and then proceeded to tell me her story.

Although the block was in a beautiful subdivision called Lakewood Estate, the person who had purchased it originally had fallen on hard times and could no longer complete the payment for it. As it had originally been marketed as part of a government promotion, it had to be legally sold now at the original price rather than its current market value. Margaret had been up praying that morning and had felt to drive down into that area. It was an area she had brought to my attention several times before and we had loved the locality due to its close proximity to a beautiful lake. However, knowing the retail value of the land in that area, I had never seriously considered it as a possibility.

As she drove into the subdivision, she noticed a man placing a 'for sale' sign on that block of land. It had only become available that morning and he was the manager of the marketing company. Margaret proceeded to place what must have sounded to him like a ridiculous offer and insisted that he submit it to the government agency involved in selling the block. She was simply the very first one to do so, and to our amazement, a few days later, he rang to say the block was ours. We placed a small deposit on it and then we got on our knees praying again!

YOU DID What?!

It was then that another friend of ours, John Steele, felt impressed in prayer that we should contact a certain builder concerning the building of a home. We made the appointment and went to see him. We found him to be a fine Christian man and during a two hour appointment, we talked only a brief time about the home as he seemed much more interested in the ministry we were involved in. At the close of the interview, he glanced sideways at his partner and then proclaimed, "Right! Now we get you into a home!" We explained that we only had a very small amount of money and could not afford a normal deposit. We went on to explain about our self-supporting, itinerant lifestyle with no steady salary and that we would not be able to secure a mortgage. His reply was simply, "Let me deal with all of that." And he did. We contributed a mere $13,000 and somehow, the Holy Spirit and our newly found friend arranged for all the necessary. Our miracle had arrived!

When we got home, I got aside in my study, closed the door and celebrated with praise and an Irish jig!

But it didn't end there. Again and again he would ask Margaret the question, "What would you really like if money was not an option?" Margaret told him about her dream for an oak kitchen, and he replied, "I'll take care of that!" We mentioned a sundeck and he replied, "I'll take care of that!". We lost count of the number of extras we ended up with, without paying a single cent for them. We loved that home and lived in it for approximately 8 years. But what is the point of the story?

God is no man's debtor.

The provision of that home had started long before we recognised it as such.

Prior to us leaving New Zealand, a Christian trust had made a decision to give us a large sum of money. In recognition of the fact that we had previously sold our home and put the money into the building programme of the church, they had decided to give us the sum of $25,000. In those days, that was a huge amount of money. However, after praying about it, Margaret and I both felt the Lord tell us to give the money away to another couple who did not have their own home. With our own considerable needs at that time, it was a major decision to make and one which would be very hard for others to understand who knew our situation.

We see now, in hindsight, that God was simply once again getting us to sow the seed for a time of reaping ahead. As in the natural laws of His creation, God works with us according to the spiritual laws He has placed within His Kingdom - for every time of reaping ahead, God must introduce opportunities for us to sow now.

Living this life of faith has taught us two principle things:

(1) That the spiritual law in 2 Corinthians 9 is totally non-negotiable to the Lord. The greatness of His provision is drawn to those of a generous heart. *Having a generous heart*

(2) That true financial freedom and joy in living comes from pouring your heart and substance into the lives of others. I cannot possibly describe to you the sheer delight that Margaret and I get at seeing God meet the need of another through some act of obedience on our part. Then, on top of that, we have the wonderful anticipation of His future miraculous supply. It is the way life is meant to be lived!

With today's talk of economic recession and restraint, many of God's people have lost sight of these principles and are now living in a state of anxiety and concern, causing them to restrain their generosity towards others. It is so sad to see them cutting off God's future abundance by living in that manner. I am not talking about reckless irresponsibility, but rather the heart attitude which is always looking to give. If all one can afford is a dollar and it is given with the right

YOU DID What?!

motivation, I guarantee you that the next time God gives them the opportunity, they will have $10 to give. And, if they maintain their joy and obedience in doing so, the day will come when they will be giving away vastly more than that! The key is the selfless motivation of the heart.

The Key TO giving - is Selfless Motivation of the heart

In obedience to His directive to leave New Zealand, we had given away what could have been our deposit on a home and then given up our home and sold it at the most illogical moment. It was against all human reasoning to do so. Consequently, we had surrendered any human possibility of us getting back into a home of our own again in the foreseeable future. Friends, true obedience is unconditional, and it does not depend upon a presumed outcome. It does not have to be either logical or reasonable. If the Lord had asked us to rent for the next 30 years, that would have been fine by us.

I should insert here that in all these years of being under Father's love and command, Margaret and I have not had one moment of being in debt (other than a normal house mortgage). He is an incredibly faithful Provider.

I have found that true joy and satisfaction is not in the result, but in the steps of obedience that take you there. I am also certain that this is what brings joy to the heart of our Father.

Chapter Thirty

BACON, EGGS AND A NEW FUTURA

One morning the pig awoke with an inspired thought which he shared with his friend the hen, "We must make the farmer a cooked breakfast this morning and it must be exactly what he asks for!"

"Are you really sure?", asked the hen.

"Absolutely! I have a conviction about it!", declared the pig with great authority.

So the two of them went and spoke with the farmer and this was his reply, "Bacon and eggs, please."

"Great!", said the hen. "That is a sacrifice I am willing to make."

"No way!", said the pig. "For you, that is just an offering. For me, that is total commitment!" It was about then that the pig realised he did not hold a conviction at all, but merely a most negotiable persuasion.

One cannot live a life of true biblical faith without living a life of strong convictions.

The very word *faith* in the Greek language (pistis) is literally translated 'an absolute conviction born out of hearing'. It is only out of hearing from God and forging a conviction that a thing is so, which enables us to live this Christian life with confidence and boldness of spirit. Such convictions must be strongly established on the Word of God and the voice of the Holy Spirit speaking directly into our hearts. His daily voice will always be in accordance with His already established Word.

Although the vast majority of our convictions will be forged out of sound biblical study, they will not become truly ours until they are tested. And even when we have established them as part of our ongoing lifestyle, there will be times when they will come under assail. The greater the provocation of our circumstances to do otherwise, the stronger that conviction will be forged into our spirit.

It was another one of those rare occasions when Margaret had not come with me on a ministry trip. We had now been in Australia for nearly 2 years and were persevering with our old Magna. Margaret informed me that it was now thoroughly sick and needed hundreds of dollars worth of repairs, money which we just simply did not have. It was a Thursday evening.

Upon arriving home, I got aside in my office for a time of prayer and almost immediately the name of a businessman in New Zealand came to my mind. As it was someone I had not heard from for a long time, I was amazed at how clearly his name had come to me. I went out and shared this with Margaret who then reminded me in no uncertain terms: "I thought you had a conviction about not telling people about this particular need!" Ouch. She was of course completely correct, and I returned to my office to continue my conversation with the Lord. "You are obviously testing me at this time. You know my conviction will not allow me to ring him and tell him of our need, so I ask you to now speak to him in New Zealand, even as you are speaking to me here in Melbourne."

The following morning, the phone rang. I couldn't believe my ears! It was his voice on the other end! After a brief moment of greeting, he got directly to the point.

"Well, David, what is it? I was praying last night and God told me that you had a need and I was the one who had to meet it." My reply was idiotic to say the least. "I have a conviction about not telling people about this present need." His exact words were, "What! Don't you go wasting my time and playing the old lady with me! You have a need and I am to meet it so will you please tell me what it is!"

I felt like a little scolded boy. "Our car is in need of repairs, and I need a few hundred dollars to fix it." "Okay! Now, really, was that so hard? How much is the car worth? How much will a new Ford cost you? What is the difference between the two?" I tried to accurately estimate and gave him the figure of $20,000 (bearing in mind that was 15 years ago). "Fine, it will be in your bank account by the end of the week!"

And that was the end of the conversation.

I was now driving a new Ford Futura with cruise control, and once again marvelling at the greatness of God's provision. When we left

New Zealand we had to sell our car, an older imported Toyota (with leather seats and cruise control) which I had really loved driving. Once again, let me declare that our Father is no man's debtor.

However, I am thoroughly convinced that if I had reached for the telephone that Thursday night and rang him myself, the outcome would have been entirely different. Friends, convictions are only as strong as the pressures that are placed upon them. It is in times when circumstances seem to leave us with no way out that we discover whether or not we have a convenient persuasion or a non-negotiable conviction.

Non Negotiable Conviction

I remember another occasion in which the Lord had made it clear that I was not supposed to advertise a particular need in any of our newsletters, etc. We had come to a particularly challenging time financially and I was travelling in a car with a newly found friend who was a successful businessman. To this very day, I cannot remember what it was I said to him, but I will never forget his reply, "Don't you ever hint to me! You either do not tell me your need or you come out openly and ask me."

I was mortified that I had crossed that line and yet so grateful I had done so with a friend who was willing to be honest with me and confront me with it. I apologised to my friend and, of course, repented when I got home.

Up until that time, I was totally unaccustomed to being around business people who had money, and I was realising that God was using them to test my convictions. It is so hard to build good credibility, and yet so very easy to lose it with an undisciplined remark. It was God's grace which allowed me to make that remark in the company of one who would not be adversely affected by it. He remains a close friend to this day, but the conviction stays in place: "Ask, or do not ask, but do not hint!" If you want to walk as a man or woman of integrity, that is very good advice to take.

For any who feels such advice is contra to my previously stated conviction of not expressing one's need - a conviction is individual and personal, whereas good advice can be wisdom to us all.

The issue is one of obedience. On those occasions in which the Lord has given the clear directive, *"Do not tell people about this"*, then silence is the conviction held, no matter how enticing the circumstances become. In the absence of such a clear directive, godly advice (such as my friend's) is wisdom.

YOU DID What?!

Chapter Thirty One

SIXTEEN LECTURES A WEEK

Our acceptance into the church family at Waverley Christian Fellowship (now CityLife Church) was wonderful. As a family, we began to make friends and our children were obviously delighted to be fully involved.

Under the senior leadership of initially Kevin Conner and subsequently his son, Mark, we knew we had found a place of divine appointment, and that we, as a family, could make this our spiritual home. The love for the Word of God, the honouring of the Holy Spirit, the integrity, and the consistently high moral standards, gave us all a sense of security.

YOU DID *What?!*

Opportunities for me to minister into that congregation on several Sundays were wonderfully blessed and the people were always most responsive.

Not long after the baton was passed from Kevin to Mark, I was asked by Mark to establish and run a course for existing and emerging leaders. We called it "Leadership Training College", and it ran for four days a week for 20 weeks.

Oh, how I loved those days! The hunger of those attending, the sense of God's grace as I was sharing, the counselling, the seeking of God and preparing for session after session, the organising of guest lecturers; it all was something that I could hurl myself into with a passion. But by far the greatest joy was seeing the transformation taking place in people's lives, and the forging of friendships that were to continue well after the course was finished.

The Leadership Training College continued for four years. At the end of that time, with Mark's approval and using the WCF premises, I continued the course under our own ministry but reduced it to a five-week term. There were no guest lecturers and I did the entire course, except for the four or five lectures that Margaret took. She spoke on the vitally important subjects of marriage and family, and still powerfully ministers on those subjects today.

With 16 lectures a week for five weeks, that gave me almost 80 lectures on the subject of leadership. It was a time of intense learning for me as well as those attending. This course went for a further two years.

As our relationships within that local church continued to strengthen, Mark eventually asked me to sit in on the eldership meetings as a guest member. This I did for several years and was able to observe the godly and biblical way in which even the most difficult of subjects were handled. Those were treasured times, and I must admit I miss them greatly.

After several years of attending those meetings, I, along with Kevin Conner and one or two others, was graciously asked to make way for some new blood; our season in that capacity had come to an end. However, we continued in good fellowship and remained involved until recently when the Lord clearly gave us direction to make Planetshakers City Church our new local church. Our relationship with Mark and the team at CityLife remains as one of mutual respect and appreciation.

As new members of Planetshakers, we have been received with love, honour and affection. Russell and Sam Evans (senior pastors of the church) have gone out of their way to ensure that we feel the strength of their acceptance and support. We are so very grateful.

Being part of a wonderful local church family has been absolutely vital for us as a prophetic ministry. I firmly believe that every itinerant minister should be established in a local church and have positive relationships with the leadership team.

Kevin Conner continues to play the role of a spiritual father to myself and our prophetic team and his input into my own life personally is invaluable. To us all, he is an outstanding example of the Christian life, and we are deeply privileged to call Kevin and his wife, Rene, our friends.

Chapter Thirty Two

LAKES AND SCENIC WALKS

Although we loved our home, we were continually drawn towards the South Eastern suburbs and felt the Lord desired us to move out into that area. In keeping with my passion for being near water and going for walks, God showed us a beautiful subdivision called Berwick Springs which once again had a beautiful lake. Another bonus was that all our children lived in that area.

We put our home at Knox up for sale at a reasonable price, but did not receive any offers whatsoever. Then one Sunday morning after the service, a friend of ours, who was considered very wise in financial matters, said to me, "Whatever you do, do not sell that home at Knox!" I explained to him that of course we had to sell the home as we would need the proceeds from that to purchase the other house. He insisted that God would make another way for us to proceed. A few days later, another friend of ours in business gave us exactly the same advice. And a few days after that, a third one repeated it. Quite obviously God was speaking to us and requiring from us another new level of faith.

We decided to believe God for some more miracles and to rent out the home in Knox. We got an amazingly high rent for it but still had to make up a shortfall in order to pay the mortgage, which was an added expense to believe God for. At that time we had only just been meeting our monthly expenses with no surplus, but we knew it was time for a major stretch in our own capacity to believe God.

We bought the new home in Berwick Springs and lived there for 3½ years. During that time there was not one occasion on which we did not pay both our mortgages, and on time! Often the provision would come in with one minute to go. Miracles of provision are not the real issue, obedience is.

I must insert here a wonderful thought.

It is a tragedy that so many Christians today consider God to be impersonal and not interested in the finer details of their lives. They think as long as it is some sort of religious endeavour, then God is involved, but otherwise He is not interested in the human aspects of our lives. Nothing could be further from the truth. As with any loving father, He is most interested in every aspect of our lives.

With me, it has always been a desire to be close to a lake in order to have my prayer walks. I have always said that in the absence of a wind-blown beach, the beauty of a large lake with scenic walks through bushland is my first choice of a place to be when I have to gain new direction or vision from the Lord. I believe the Lord is vitally interested in that desire and He has provided it with each of our three homes, including our current one. On each occasion, the size of the lake has notably increased!

I believe it is time for us all to realise God's loving father's heart and how much He desires to be involved in not only the urgent and the intensely spiritual, but also in the human desires of His children. As in this case, our natural desires are often the result of His purpose. The Bible is clear that He formed us from our mother's womb, and so it is only reasonable to assume that the purposes He has chosen for us will dictate the natural desires He then places within us.

Back to the story…

When it came time to secure our present property for both personal and ministry needs, we had two homes to sell, not one, and the one at Knox had risen considerably in value. We previously had it on the market for $330,000 and had no interest whatsoever, and now, some three years later, hoped to sell it for something in the $370,000 - $380,000 range. The market had risen in that time, and our faith was high (or so we thought!). It certainly would have been a good price.

Once again there appeared to be an initial difficulty in marketing the property, until one day an accountant arrived and declared that he would not enter into any negotiations whatsoever but would state his price and that would be final. His offer was for $422,000! It was an incredible price for that property.

Oh, was I glad I had listened to the wise counsel of my three friends and the confirmation of the Holy Spirit at that time instead of allowing the bank balance and budget to rule. They are vital and necessary as servants, but terrible and crippling as masters.
I do not dispute the vital necessity of living wisely as a faithful stew-

ard which involves a good budget, but know the danger of allowing the apparent facts to rule over the voice of the Holy Spirit in your heart.

The safeguard for Margaret and for me has been that we have always surrounded ourselves with those whom we trust to give wise counsel. I am certainly not advocating irresponsibility. There are many today whose lives are in financial disaster because they did not listen to good stewardship and sound advice. I believe that good stewardship demands self-discipline, and that any instructions God gives us will be confirmed in ways that do not leave it to speculation.

Just as God gives us evangelists and teachers to instruct us in biblical principles, so too He has given to us those who are wise in financial and business matters. Too many spiritual leaders have the faulty notion that to ask advice from qualified business and financial consultants is to somehow betray their reliance on the Holy Spirit. They seem to forget that the same God who made them a pastor also made that person a business leader and gifted them accordingly. I have always sought to balance daring faith with an acknowledgement of the need for wise counsel according to the wisdom of the proverb: *In the multitude of counsellors there is safety* [see Proverbs 11:14].

But make sure that those you surround yourself with are men and women of prayer and faith. In appreciating their natural experience and qualifications, we never lose sight of the fact that they must be men and women who also hear clearly from the Holy Spirit. We want the advice of highly qualified people, but highly qualified people who have an intimacy with Father's heart and a solid Christian faith. Men and women who are not intimidated by natural sight and the prevailing anxieties of the day.

Chapter Thirty Three

LIONS AND HUNGRY PEOPLE

Whenever I would think about Africa, I would think about lions, giraffes and safaris. But, not being a natural born missionary, I never had a desire to go there. Heat, sweat and dust have never been my favourite environment. That was all about to change.

It was the mid-90s, and Margaret and I began to feel strongly drawn to that great continent. We opened dialogue with Kent Hodge who directed the All Nations for Christ Bible Institute in Benin City, Nigeria (attached to the ministry of Archbishop Benson Idahosa).

Plans were made and we flew out.

We were accompanied by two loyal friends who had sacrificially taken a year off work to help us in our ministry as volunteers. Their help and assistance to us at that time was huge, and we were (and continue to be) so very grateful for two such servant-hearted people.

The ministry there proved to be incredibly fruitful, and Margaret and I had the privilege of ministering to 'ministers in training'. The 'classroom' (with desks for each one) was huge and there were almost 1200 students! Their hunger and response was amazing as they clapped, cheered and broke out in celebration as a truth was seen and embraced.

Now for a rewind … Let us go back to the months prior to leaving on that trip.

I had contacted a New Zealand pastor, who had gone to live in Tanzania as a missionary, by the name of Alan Stevenson. He and his wife, Lynda, were pioneering a wonderful work that today flourishes in that nation and throughout Africa. Margaret and I felt that we were to go and encourage them en route to Nigeria, and that arrangement was made.

Early one morning, the Lord awoke me with a strong and clear commission: *"Gather the leaders of churches together in Tanzania."* It was so totally out of the blue that I had to pray it through over several days. When I submitted it to Margaret, she confirmed that she felt this was indeed from the Lord.

Alan informed me that there was only one way this gathering could become a possibility and that was to pay for all the costs of those who would attend. He explained that this would involve covering the cost of travel, accommodation and food for all concerned. Alan thought approximately 50 might attend and they would be significant leaders in that area. Even with that number, the cost of meeting all their expenses, on top of our own expenses of getting there, was huge. We had to consider airfares, accommodation and of course lack of income, as we would not be receiving any honorariums during that time.

We looked at our bank balance, and we had the princely sum of $1150. Obviously it was only a fraction of what we needed, but we knew we had heard a clear word from God and committed ourselves to go. That's right about the moment when someone released the handbrake on the roller coaster!

After all the arrangements were made and the tickets were booked, an email arrived and it was from Alan. He informed me that the 50 was now going to be 100. Though realising that our faith step had now grown considerably, we agreed to say yes. The next email put the figure at 200. The next one put it at 300. The next one put it at 400. We finally peaked at 470! By now, I had lost track of the zeros we had been adding to the cost and my mind was starting to go numb.

Showing incredible self-discipline and restraint, I walked quietly into my office and closed the door. And then I hollered, "Father! I need a whole lot of money! What should I do?!" I was used to taking steps of faith, but this really was enormous in the light of our circumstances at that time. The size of the miracle seemed overwhelming, but I knew that we had prayed it through, heard from God, and were committed.

Finally I heard His voice say, *"Take $1000 and give it to that other needy itinerant minister."*

What?! I reminded the Lord that it was me who needed the money! Remember now, we only had $1150 in the bank. I have found there are times that the things God asks of us are not at all reasonable.

YOU DID What?!

But, then again, He does not have to be reasonable. He is God!

I shared with Margaret what I felt the Lord had said to me and was met with what was now a predictable response, "If that is what the Lord has said then that is exactly what we will do." Oh, how I thank the Lord for a wife who is filled with faith and has never flinched from obeying a clear directive from Him. I firmly believe that any lesser mortal would have gone completely insane living the kind of life which God has called us to live. We gave away the $1000, and now we had the huge sum of $150 to fund the entire trip and to live and feed our family.

To cut a very long story short, every expense was paid for and the final $2000 came to us the night before we flew out. The trip itself was not only incredibly fruitful for the Kingdom but opened up a whole new era of ministry expression for Margaret and myself. We have since been into Africa numerous times including Tanzania, Nigeria, Uganda, Kenya and Ethiopia. Our daughter Rachael and her husband Steve with their two sons have been missionaries in both Tanzania and Ethiopia, and have only recently returned to live in Melbourne.

Friends, I say it yet again: miracles are not the problem, obedience is.

Chapter Thirty Four

NO CHEWING THE LOCUSTS!

H e came thundering out of the desert, clothed in skins and chomping the heads off locusts. John the Baptist must have been quite a sight!

As I have observed the prophetic movement, it has often saddened me to see the discredit brought to it by those who believe that it is still acceptable to be a little weird. They seem to forget that John the Baptist was an Old Testament prophet and not intended as an indication that 21st century prophets should wear skins and eat locusts!

I have a passion to de-spook the prophetic. In fact, spooky people make me very nervous!

As I look back over 40 plus years of serving the Lord (most of those as a prophet), I am so grateful that the Lord has led me from the initial years of great intensity (and, at times, outright religiosity) to being able to function in His grace in a more relaxed manner. These days I see the giving of a prophetic word as more of a conversation than a thundering declaration. After all, it is simply the Holy Spirit communicating the heart of Father to His children.

God cares about people. He loves His children. He is protective, caring, encouraging, challenging and, on occasions, lovingly confronting. He will warn, instruct, mould and fashion us to be all that He has created us to be, but He will never be brutal, harsh or cutting in His remarks. He is our Father and He loves us. I believe that the responsibility of prophetic ministries today is to not only communicate His Word, but His heart.

I never cease to marvel at our Father's wonderful commitment to those of us who love Him. I consistently have people communicating with me concerning a prophetic word I gave them, in some cases, many years ago. From deeply personal words to instructions concerning the purchase of property, confirmation of dreams and desires, warnings concerning the potential of a church split and how to constructively deal with it, comfort in the times of crisis, and the Word of the Lord to a city. I have had the privilege of delivering such messages to individuals in a car park or an office corridor, to pastors and leaders, to politicians, and to non-Christian men and women who were convinced that God was not real.

I have ministered in countless nations around the world, but I can never recall a single occasion in which there was the need to be harsh, brutal or publicly exposing. On those rare occasions where sin did have to be confronted, God always orchestrated circumstances so I could speak with that person individually and in private (with the inclusion of their pastor if vitally necessary). Why? Because God is not into damaging people. He is into rescuing people with the revelation of His love. When someone knows that He could have exposed them, but chose not to, they are often overwhelmed by His caring for them in their sinful state. And it is His love that brings them to repentance.

Although this book was never intended to become primarily an instruction on the prophetic, it would be impossible to tell the story of my life journey without mentioning one or two occasions in which God's love so wonderfully intervened. Here are a few that stand out in my memory, and the principle I discovered at that time I can now pass on to you.

I have already told you of the event in which Violet Kitely prophesied that I would be a teacher of the Word and that it took seven years to come to pass.

If God speaks to you in a similar manner at any time, and you find it hard to connect that prophetic word with your present reality, then put it on the shelf and await God's timing in bringing it to pass. Neither dismiss it, nor strive to bring it to pass.

Another occasion that illustrates the same principle was when I was speaking at a ministers' conference in Northern Queensland many years ago. After the conference, I stayed on to preach in the local church on the Sunday morning and assumed that those present were local church members. I gave a word to a couple sitting near the back concerning turbulent times coming in their church environment and how to wisely deal with it. I listed several steps that would ensure the damage would be minimal at that time.

Years later, they told me that they had rejected the word as their local church environment had never been healthier. They were associate pastors on the full-time team and could see no application of the word whatsoever. Almost a year later, their senior minister had to be stood down from ministry due to previous moral failures which had come to light, and the whole church was terribly shaken. They then remembered the word I had given to them in Northern Queensland and assembled the elders together to listen to it. That Sunday, the eldership played it to the entire church, who wholeheartedly embraced it. In walking through the several steps of instruction that God had given to them in that word, the church was able to handle that crisis with a minimum loss of people.

Then there was the time when I was being driven to an appointment to meet someone for the first time. All I knew about him was that he was a respected minister, and that he and I were being offered the opportunity to serve on a Board of Advisors together.

As we approached the car park, the Holy Spirit spoke very clearly to me concerning this man. Knowing that there were other ministers present and that my credibility was on the line, it was a scary moment. As we were introduced, he offered me his hand but before he could get into conversation with me, I immediately told him that I had a word to deliver, which was, "You are to go back to the place of your birth, the place of the well, and take up the responsibility there." He was polite enough not to tell me I was a total fruitcake and received the word even though it did not appear to apply at the time. Some weeks later, he received a call to take up the position of senior minister in another city and in another nation. He later told me he would not have given that invitation another thought if it had not been for the word that I had shared with him.

God knows when we need extra evidence that it is He who is speaking to us. The significance of the word was as follows: the church which had offered him the invitation was in fact, the church where he got born again, that is the place of his spiritual birth. The name of the city literally translated from the native language was "the place of the well". How wonderfully detailed our Father can be!

He accepted the invitation and today is the most successful senior minister of that local church and highly respected in that nation. He also has become a great friend to Margaret and I.

The Bible is quite clear that God is not the author of confusion. Whereas I have a conviction about obeying God instantly and fully, I have an equally strong conviction that we must be convinced that it is God who is speaking. The boldness of our confidence in the days that lie ahead and the tests that assuredly will come will be determined by how clearly we believe we have heard from the Holy Spirit. If you are genuinely unsure of the nature of the word you have received, then our Father is not offended when you continue to pray concerning it, and He will find a way to confirm it clearly to you.

Most often prophecy is confirmation, but there are such occasions when it is God's loving intervention for a time that He sees is yet to come. He is ever vigilant, and instinctively protective of His people. There is no safer place than to be in His service, living a fully surrendered life. Fear can grip our planet and uncertainty the hearts of men, but you can face the future with confidence and peace of heart, knowing that your loving Father is ordering your steps and will intervene at any time you need it.

The secret is in living a fully surrendered life and walking in intimacy with His heart.

A few years ago, I had been teaching a group of pastors on the principles of simple obedience to God's voice. On the way home I was mouthing my disappointment to the Lord. "Lord, I don't understand. This is all so simple. Why can they not just accept the simplicity of it? You speak, we hear, we obey, You bless. What is difficult about that?" I was on a roll until, in a brief moment when I paused to catch my breath, He spoke: *"What about the car?!"*

The car! I knew exactly what He meant.

For months I had been arranging the most amazing lease deal on a new Holden. It was at a cheaper price than all of my associates in the ministry had been able to get and I got to choose colour, trim, etc. The cost each month was considerably less than the depreciation on our two existing cars, one of which was really old. It was great stewardship and we couldn't wait for it all to go through. My sons were already lining up for their first spin and I talked freely with fellow ministers about how such a deal could be done if you were Irish and spiritual enough. Most of my world knew about 'the car'.

So He speaks.
"What about the car?!"
"But Lord, it is stewardship!"
"I want the car!"
"Father, I have told everyone about this."
"I want the car."
"Do you have any idea as to the depreciation on those two cars in my garage?"
"I want the car."
"I have signed everything. I am about to get delivery."
"I want the car."
"Lord, I am going to look like an idiot!"
"I want the cotton-pickin' car!!!"

I drove up my driveway wrestling. Maybe it wasn't God's voice. Maybe this was the devil trying to do me out of this great provision. Maybe I was just trying to prove spirituality by being a martyr. And, of course, I really would look like an idiot.

The next morning I had to prepare for a meeting. The Heavens were as brass. "Hello, are You still up there?" Nothing. "Yeah, I know. You want the cotton-pickin' car!" I had finally come to a place of surrender. I rang up and cancelled the car.

I told Margaret and the kids. Some responses were kinder than others, but when I got to my colleagues, some were outright insensitive! Then, to top it all off, the next day I see the exact car and colour slowly cruise its way past my house! Now that just isn't fair!

Well, a few days later the phone rang and it was a businessman I knew. The results of that conversation was the selling my two existing vehicles and being put in the driver's seat of the latest Ford with cruise control. This vehicle won the "Car of the Year" award and it was costing me exactly zero per month. A few days after that, the phone goes again and it is another businessman. The result of that call was that I now had his XR6 Turbo to drive for nearly a year! I was almost too embarrassed to drive up to a meeting in it. In the space of a few weeks I had gone from two cars needing to be replaced to having two brand new Fords in my garage.

Is God interested in the tin and the wheels? No. He is interested in obedience. One of the simple statements I had shared with the pastors that day was what I believe is the sum total of living a successful Christian life: "Hear and Obey". That really is it. Pay the price to hear His voice and then have the courage to do what He says without mucking it up with a lot of good sound logic and reason.

It was just one statement which could have so easily been put aside or reasoned out: "What about the car?" It was a moment that had to be seized. That car was another one of my 'Isaac' moments. We have all had such moments and we will all have more of them. The challenge is what we do in such moments. If our response is spontaneous and obedience is instant, we will find a miracle is on its way.

YOU DID What?!

Chapter Thirty Five

THE LION ROARS!

Early in 1998, an old foe came back to haunt me. I once again began to feel those familiar pains in the chest and when out walking with Margaret, I would often get short of breath. This led to a visit to a heart specialist, who then told me I would have to have an angiogram, which I did on 23rd March 1998. We returned to the heart specialist on 1st May 1998 to get the results.

As we drove into the car park, the ever faithful Holy Spirit spoke into my heart and said, *"Bind the power of the words you are about to hear."* Margaret and I held hands in the car and did exactly that. We then proceeded to the waiting room for the longest 30 minutes I've ever had in my entire life. As the heart specialist ushered us into his office and began to tell us the results, I was so very glad that the Holy Spirit had spoken to us in the car park.

"All of your major arteries and most of your subsidiary arteries have multiple blockages." With that statement he then proceeded to show us graphically the condition of my arteries. The printout of my arteries was just a mass of Xs and numbers: 75% blocked, 60% blocked, 93% blocked, 80% blocked, 92% blocked, 85% blocked, and the list continued. Margaret, who has a medical background, immediately asked him what could be done. He replied that angioplasty would kill me and that a bypass was probably not going to be successful due to the number of blockages involved. He said that, though the thought of a bypass would be kept as a last resort one day to save my life, the outcome could not be guaranteed. It certainly was too risky unless there was no alternative. The bottom line was that there was nothing they could do for me surgically to improve my condition.

He then proceeded to graciously but firmly tell me what my new lifestyle should look like: no lifting anything heavy, don't get too excited, be careful about strenuous activity or lifestyle, live a life that does not demand any stress. I honestly cannot remember the exact terms he used but that is the general spirit of what he said.

He was talking to someone who had always lived life at a million miles an hour! He obviously had no idea about the nature of itinerant ministry, let alone an Irish one! My mind began to think of what my normal 12 months would look like in a given year. Did this now mean that my ministry life was over? A myriad of thoughts were bombarding my mind. And then I remembered the car park! My God was still in charge.

As we drove home I tried to reassure Margaret as best I could, knowing that such news was devastating for any wife to hear. I think people do not realise fully how hard it is on the spouse of one who is going through a major physical difficulty and often reserve their prayer and comfort just for the individual.

The following morning I was in prayer in my study and reminded the Lord that in previous times of crisis He had always given me a clear word. It is so wonderful to know that He is faithful in such times. As I stopped to listen, He spoke just one word: *"Samson."* It was so clear, but my response was anything but appropriate: "Samson! He is not one of my favourite people in the Bible! Why Samson?!" His quiet but definite voice spoke again: *"Samson!"*

As I got my Bible and looked for the Book of Judges, it fell open at the exact page that He desired me to look at. One verse immediately leapt off the page to me. It was Judges 14:5 ... *a lion came roaring against him!* I said, "Yes, Lord! That's exactly how I feel!" He said, *"Good! Now read the next verse."* Here is what it said: *And the Spirit of the Lord came mightily upon him, and he tore the lion apart as one would have torn apart a young goat, though he had nothing in his hands.*

Friends, all I can tell you is in that moment, all anxiety and concern completely left my spirit as the presence of Lord filled the room. He then proceeded to show me that what I had been preaching for many years on spiritual authority and taking dominion now had to be brought into reality in my own life. He assured me that as I walked daily in His grace and took authority over the condition, it would not kill me as long as I walked in His will and purpose. The feelings that flooded into my heart at that time were a mixture of confidence, boldness and great joy. It was as if He had filled my heart with an unreasonable faith!

I ran out to Margaret and we prayed and rejoiced together.

When I returned to my office, the Lord spoke a most remarkable statement to me: *"I will do in and through your physical body that which I desire to see achieved, through you, in My spiritual body."* Over the next few months, the Holy Spirit continually spoke to me concerning the principles which allow a man or woman to walk in true spiritual authority. That experience has birthed a number of vital messages for the Body of Christ on the subject of 'The Overcomer'.

One day when I was rejoicing over the impact the message of 'The Overcomer' was having upon God's people, the Lord reminded me that Samson had gone back to the carcass of that lion and found it filled with a swarm of bees and honey.

In verse 14 of that same chapter, Samson gives a riddle: *Out of the eater came something to eat, and out of the strong came something sweet.*

Two principles of great significance came to me during that time:

(1) If we respond God-ward in our times of crisis, the Lord will honour His word and will turn all things for good; and

(2) In order to proclaim the message with ultimate effectiveness we must first become the message.

I would have to say that the vast majority of life-giving messages that God has given me to preach have come out of times of personal challenge and difficulty. When we understand that principle, such events and seasons do not become a threat but the great and awesome opportunities that God intended them to be. A sword forged with ease will break at the first blow, but a sword forged in fire will pierce the heart of the enemy and be a weapon of God's conquest.

Since that declaration of death and gloom over me, I have experienced the best 14 years of my life! I exercise freely and work out with weights; I live a full-on ministry schedule; and Margaret and I have hiked in the Swiss Alps with packs on our backs! I have not experienced any angina for over a decade and feel fitter and fuller of life than at any previous time.

Let me quickly add here that this wake up call drew my attention to the issue of looking after the body that God gave me, and I made substantial changes to both my diet and my lifestyle. I honour Him by honouring the gift of life that He has given me.

Friends, do you have a lion roaring? Is there a devourer that dares to declare your time is finished and that the promises of God for you can now not ever be fulfilled? I am here to tell you that he is a liar, a thief, and one that Jesus gloriously defeated. That which he has sent against you for evil, God will turn for good. The very weapon that he chooses to attack you with will become the instrument of your future ministry and victory in the lives of others. Do not resent your situation, but look into it for the principle of life that God has placed there. I know that as you do, the shadows will draw back and the sun will begin to shine again.

YOU DID *What?!*

Chapter Thirty Six

THE MIRACLE OF AVONWOOD

I t was 2004 and once again Margaret and I were in East Africa.

We went out to dinner with Alan & Lynda in Arusha, Tanzania. During the conversation that night, Alan asked me these questions (which I think every reader should now ask themselves), "David, if God allowed you to choose absolutely anything, what would you want to do with rest of your life above all valid ministry expressions you are involved in? What would be your priority?"

After munching my way through a few mouthfuls of wildebeest steak, I found myself saying, "I would want to mentor potential and existing ministers and leaders and run courses that would strengthen them in their calling." It was quite a defining moment.

The following morning, the Lord woke me at 4:30 and challenged me to pursue a more deliberate and proactive attitude concerning speaking into the lives of pastors and leaders.

I, of course, responded and said I would pursue that goal as soon as we returned home. He then told me that He would empower us to purchase a property which would be able to facilitate both our own home and the ministry centre. Then came the spiritual video - scene after scene flashed through my mind of trees and lawns and that which could be seen as we were looking out of various windows. It really was amazing!

Believing firmly in the principle that once God has clearly spoken, we must position ourselves to possess that which is promised, Margaret and I set out to find the property as soon as we returned. Because of the wise counsel of our brethren three years previously, we now had two houses to sell for a new venture. However, with a substantial mortgage on both, it soon became apparent that it would be nowhere near enough. (At that time we were also renting offices in a local church.) It would mean raising a mortgage beyond anything we had ever previously considered. But the bottom line was that God had clearly spoken and therefore, He obviously was going to make a way.

For some 18 months we looked. Property after property was presented to us, but nowhere could we find the exact one God had shown me while in Arusha. On one occasion, we found a property which was almost what God had shown me and could have become close to it if we had done enough hard work with it. By this time I had grown weary of looking and was eager to get the vision underway, and began to reason that I should not be too exacting. The property itself was certainly a nice property and beyond anything that Margaret and I had previously considered living in. It was almost perfect. Almost.

Once again, I was to thank the Lord for wonderful friends and good counsel. One of my newly acquired board members asked me the question, "Is this the exact properly God laid upon your heart? Personally, I believe you are settling for second best and that God has something better for you." God was bringing me back into focus. A few days later a friend of mine, who was a well-recognised prophet, gave me a word that clearly confirmed. We were back out searching again.

One morning, the real estate agent said that she had a property to show me even though it had been sold at that time. She explained that the sale had not gone unconditional yet and therefore felt free to show us the property.

We had with us our lifelong friend and intercessor, Jacky, visiting from New Zealand. The moment we drove down the driveway, we realised that this was an amazing place! It was an acre in size and the trees and lawns looked exactly as God had shown me nearly two years previously. As the agent showed us through that beautiful home, its outdoor entertainment area, its swimming pool, the additional three bedroom cottage, and the huge games room with timber floors, we agreed that this indeed was where God wanted us to live and have our ministry base.

I made an offer that the agent felt was too low. She also reminded me that it had already been sold, though conditionally. Inside my heart I knew none of this information was relevant whatsoever as God had already given it to us nearly 2 years before, at 4:30 one wonderful morning in Africa.

Some weeks later, the agent rang to tell us that the other sale had fallen through and that our offer had been accepted. As we rejoiced together we also realised that this was where great miracles had to start happening again, and soon. Our home in Knox had not sold yet, and therefore we had to find an initial mortgage of $540,000, but that figure would be reduced considerably by the equity we had in that house. The net mortgage was eventually reduced down to $370,000. We were informed that our monthly mortgage repayments would go from $1150 a month to $3350! Realising that we had only just been breaking even for the previous year, the difference of $2200 a month seemed like $2 million a month! We had no idea where it would come from, other than the fact that God would not have brought us to this property without knowing how He was going to supply for it. We signed all the papers and went beyond the point of no return.

I know that some people at the time must have thought us to be crazy or irresponsible, but when I enquired of the Lord in prayer, I was reminded of the story of Peter walking on water. I had often asked congregations who would like to walk on water just one time in their life. I would always receive an overwhelming response, but would follow it up with the statement that the real issue was not who wants to walk on water, but who is willing to get out of the boat!

It is, of course, critical to place Peter's 'walking on water' incident in context. He was responding to a clear command from Jesus: *"Come."* Peter had first asked the question, "Lord, if it be You, bid me to come." [see Matthew 14:28-29].

Writing about the way in which Father has so miraculously provided for our needs, although written to inspire awe in Him, was a vulnerability. The Church already has too many irresponsible people who feel that God is an ATM and that the rules of obedience and stewardship are irrelevant. My story is not meant to fuel that imbalance.

The key to miraculous provision is living a life under divine command. My stories should be seen in the context of living a life of intimacy and submission to Father's will and to those He has placed in oversight to the Body of Christ.

My acts of boldness are not the fruit of my own desires, nor the fruit of impetuous and independent thinking. They are responses to clearly given and confirmed commands which have been witnessed to by senior spiritual advisors in my life.

I strongly believe in godly restraints and stewardship that ensure our finances reflect a life which truly honours Father and is a good witness to Him.

Having said that, it is also true that if we are living a life under divine command, there will be times when obedience demands of us steps of unreasonable faith.

Friends, everybody wants the amazing miracle testimony, but very few are willing to be in a position where that miracle is actually necessary. I believe that God is aching to be God but our humanity's desire to feel safe and secure so often shuts Him out from the opportunity to do so. Only when there is no possibility of us handling it ourselves, does God get the opportunity to do that which He alone can do.

The property in Avonwood Road was ours and we moved in with great rejoicing but with a need for an awesome and immediate miracle to pay the first mortgage payment.

Within days the phone rang and the minister of a large local church, who I had preached for only once at that time, informed me that God had spoken to him and his leadership team that they were to support us each month with a percentage of the tithe of the tithe. He knew absolutely nothing of our monetary need for the mortgage payment. The first cheque arrived five days before the first mortgage payment was due and it was in excess of $2000! And although the amount can vary from month to month, it has actually increased and it has been there every month for the last seven years and continues still.

I will say this again, friends: God is aching to be God, if we will only give Him the opportunities to be so. Dare I repeat this once more: miracles are not the challenge, obedience is.

Chapter Thirty Seven

SNOW
IN SUMMER

By 2007, Margaret and I had been married for 37 years and had spent 35 of those in full-time Christian ministry. Although we had tried to faithfully have normal holidays, it was pointed out to us that we had never had long service leave. In fact, we had never had any extended type of holiday at all.

Although our Board and our advisors all felt that this was long overdue and that Margaret and I should plan to do so in the immediate future, I knew that it was also going to take a remarkable miracle of provision. As over 80% of the total income for the entire team and global mission was coming in directly from my own ministry expression, I knew that the cost of such a holiday would not only be the direct costs but also the lack of income during that period of time. We agreed to pray about it, and indeed the Lord strongly confirmed that this should now take place.

The next question, of course, was where? The more we prayed about it and discussed it, we knew that the real desire of our hearts was to go to Europe. However, I kept putting that thought aside due to the obvious cost of a trip to that part of the world.

In my desire to be a faithful steward of God's finances, I had always felt strongly that one should do things as economically as possible and this seemed to contradict that conviction of my heart. In addition, the term of the long service leave had continued to increase to where we were now willing to accept the advice of our Board and see it extended to 10 weeks.

As I was wrestling with this one day, I felt the Lord say the following phrase into my heart: *"You will be going to take in Europe but I will be taking you there so that Europe can take you in."* The decision was made to go, but my mind would continually come back to the subject of faithful stewardship. On the outside I radiated faith to Margaret but on the inside I really needed one more confirmation. I finally blurted out to the Lord one day, "If You really want us to go Lord, then You will have to show me in a way that even I cannot argue with."

A few days later, a businessman came to me for some counsel. Two or three days after that conversation, he came to see Margaret and I and said, "Are you and Margaret going to take a decent holiday or not!" I replied that we had already decided to do that. "Good! I have business class seats around the world for both of you!" He must have wondered why there was such silence as I was, for one of the very few times in my entire life, totally speechless. I had asked God for a sign, but this was something else! We had never been offered such a thing in our entire lives, and it came within days of me asking God for His confirmation. The businessman rang back later. He had upgraded the entire journey to first class!

It was now very obvious that God's purpose was to take us to Europe, but it was equally clear that I was not to accept any ministry invitations and that this was to be a holiday. I really struggled with that thought, but knew God had spoken too clearly for me to continue to be awkward with it. We proceeded to plan the trip and to book various locations and hotels, etc.

Little did I know of the miracles that were about to take place. Margaret's Mum received her well-earned promotion and went to honour the population of Heaven with her wonderful faith and tenacity. She left a will and Margaret's part of the inheritance made a sizeable dent in the funds needed for the trip.

But that was only the beginning. By the time the 10 weeks was complete and we had returned home, we discovered that the trip had cost us absolutely nothing. We actually had more money in the bank upon our return than we had prior to the planning of the trip!

It is important for you to know that at this point of the narrative, so that all I am about to go on and say is held in that context.

Just prior to our leaving, the same businessman came to see me and said that he had supplied the tickets out of obedience to a direct command from the Lord. He then informed me that the Lord wanted to change my perception of myself and the value He placed upon the ministry that He had called me to do. He then said that on this particular trip, God would treat Margaret and me as 'royalty'. I told him not to say such things and that it was a privilege to be going at all. However, he was adamant that this was part of a process whereby God was shaking my thinking. You can now judge for yourself as I share some of the stories from those 10 weeks.

YOU DID What?!

It would not be appropriate for me to give you a day by day journal of our holiday as it would take a sizeable book all on its own. However, we saw magnificent countryside; visited castles; had an amazing River cruise from Vienna to Amsterdam on three major rivers over 13 days; walked in the Swiss Alps; took a 7-day Mediterranean cruise; visited Rome, Ephesus, Turkey; stayed in a fishing village on the coast of Italy; and heaps more! I will highlight a few of the events that will give you an idea of the degree to which God directed us and constantly intervened on our behalf.

Friends of ours had recommended a Mediterranean cruise which included places that Paul had preached in, such as Smyrna and Ephesus. We booked the same cruise, for the same cost, with the same company. For that amount, our friends received an inner cabin without any view. For exactly the same amount, we received a beautiful state room on one of the highest decks of this brand new ultra-luxury ship, with our own private balcony over the ocean! We not only walked the roads of Ephesus and wondered at the sights in Constantinople, but we travelled in style. That businessman's words were starting to ring true in my heart as I marvelled at my Father's abundant provision.

The same thing happened on the River cruise. A beautiful state room with every five-star plus luxury you could imagine. The second day of the cruise was the Captain's dinner evening and we were all supposed to wear our finest gear. As we were getting ready, a note was slipped under our door, which simply read: "The Captain would like the honour of your presence at his own table for this evening". What?! Obviously, there had been some mistake.

Upon presenting ourselves at the captain's table, we were informed that there was no mistake and that they were indeed most privileged to have us at their table. No explanation. There were only three couples invited out of the entire cruise ship, and I assumed that the other two were billionaires! With more changes of silverware than I have ever seen in my entire life and waiters in tails, we were truly treated as royalty for the rest of that night. To this day, I have no idea of why we were chosen to be at that table.

As part of the cruise, we were informed that we would attend a Mozart-Strauss concert in a huge concert hall in Vienna. As the 80 people from our cruise ship arrived in the car park, we saw that there were many other groups arriving with hundreds of people. As we were being escorted into the foyer, we were told that we did not have a choice of seat, but that we would be taken to our allocated areas.

Are you ready for this? Out of the thousands of people present that night, Margaret and I were escorted to the centre two seats on the front row!

Then we were in the Swiss Alps, and it was in the middle of summer. The weather was beautiful and people were in shorts and t-shirts. We hiked and were overawed at the magnificence of the mountains and the green valleys.

One day Margaret made this statement to me: "Just imagine what this would be like in the winter when it would be snowing." I agreed and we continued our hike but that night I laid awake in bed thinking about it. In a joking manner, I said to the Lord, "You are the Creator. You could actually make it snow in the middle of summer. It would be an amazing sight to see." I chuckled to myself and eventually fell asleep.

We woke the next morning feeling somewhat cold. As we pulled back the curtains, our eyes were met with a blaze of white! Not only was it steadily snowing but it had obviously been snowing most of the night, as it now lay thick upon the ground. We could hardly believe our eyes!

It continued to snow throughout that day much to the amazement of the locals who knew, of course, that it was supposed to be bright sunshine at that time of the year. They told us that the snow had been so heavy over that one day period that it had broken off the branches of large trees. We had actually heard some of those loud cracks and had wondered what they were.

Oh, I know that there could be a myriad of explanations for such an event taking place, but the one I have chosen is that Father took up that request from one of His children and got a huge buzz out of doing what fathers love to do.

Then there was the time we were on the coast of Italy. Margaret said it was absolutely vital that we buy some bright coloured ribbon to tie on to our suitcases so that they would stand out a little more at the airport.

After trying three shops to no avail, I realised that in such a small fishing area, no such item would be stocked anywhere. I stood in the middle of that third shop and prayed, "Father, all I need is some bright ribbon." As we stepped outside the shop onto the footpath, our eyeballs popped wide open. Bright yellow ribbon lay all over the footpath! This was the same footpath we had walked on when we went into the shop only a few minutes earlier.

One day, after walking for several hours from village to village and drinking lots of fluid, a certain human necessity was making itself screamingly obvious to me. I needed to find a bathroom and I needed to find one quickly! I looked around and could find nothing that even resembled one and urgently informed Father of my dilemma. Within seconds of me uttering that prayer, a doorway to an alleyway swung open to reveal a sign which clearly said "Toilet". It was in English!

When visiting the historic town of Gutenberg in Germany, we had the privilege of going to see the famous Gutenberg Press, the very first printing press in history. Surrounded by security and listening to the narrative, it was like being at a shrine! But then came the moment when it was announced that they were going to re-enact the original event using the original Gutenberg Press and they needed someone to operate it. Awesome!

And who do you think they chose? You got it! As I placed my hands on that invaluable piece of history, I prayed (an internal scream!) that I wouldn't muck it up or break it!

Well, a photo of the occasion along with the first page of the Book of John, which I had printed, now hangs framed on my office wall.

You may be one in a crowd of a thousand but Father's favour can still beam in on you like a heat-seeking missile!

Just one more! Pleeeeease. After all I'm Irish and its storytelling time.

Then there was the car. Before leaving Melbourne, I had booked a hire car at Edinburgh Airport for us to tour around Scotland and England. As there was just the two of us, I was careful to book a small economy vehicle that I considered good stewardship.

Upon presenting my voucher at the airport counter, I was informed by a most embarrassed young man that my car had just been hired out to another customer. Discussions then took place and I was informed that there were no cars left in that class or the next class. I was then asked the question, "For the same price, would you mind driving a new Mercedes?" Father had done it again!

I could keep going on and on and on and on. However, I will have mercy.

I have given you only a sampling of what became an almost daily occurrence. We saw more divine interventions on that one holiday than I had seen on exclusively ministry trips. Why? I believe, in part, it was to impress upon us that Father wanted us back in Europe for future ministry. It was also to build our faith for the size of the challenges He knew would lie before us over the next few years.

It also was because He is a father, and we were there in obedience and total dependence upon Him.

The following year, we returned to England and Europe as He opened doors for us to speak to groups of pastors and leaders. The next year, we returned again to speak to an increased number of pastors. And then the year after that, I had the privilege of speaking to approximately 200 pastors and leaders in Rotterdam as well as speaking at the largest church in the Netherlands.

As I am typing this, I am reminded of that which the Lord spoke to me when I was originally wrestling with the idea of taking a holiday in Europe: *"You will be going to take in Europe but I am taking you there so that Europe can take you in."*

At the risk of sounding boringly repetitive, let me again state that miracles are not the challenge. Obedience is.

I am so very grateful that I serve a God who not only cares about nations and great crusades, but hears a cry for bright ribbon, snow in summer and an English toilet sign in an isolated Italian fishing village. Life with Father can be a real buzz at times!

Chapter Thirty Eight

SOLO NO MORE

For 15 years Margaret and I had known the security of a salary as the senior ministers of a local church. Certainly those days were filled with challenges of faith, but it was always in the context of the others around us and very much a team effort. When we went out as itinerant ministers, the level of faith had to completely change.

Father, knowing what was ahead, knew that we had to come to a place of total dependence on Him. I remember well the exhortations of encouragement from so many senior ministers in New Zealand saying, "You know if you step out in faith, there will be a ground swell of financial support from around the country and your monthly support is assured. Just send out a letter letting everybody know and let us all respond." Well, we sent out the letter and waited for the incredible avalanche of finances.

The result was indeed remarkable. It was exactly zero! Out of approximately 100 letters going out, we had about four or five replies to inform us that they could not support us at this time and that they were indeed sorry. From the other 90 plus, there was this thundering silence that told us louder than any words ever could that no money was going to be coming via that means of support. We started our itinerant ministry with the support of our own local church of $100 a month (1988, of course!) and knew that God was sending us a very clear message: He and He alone is to be our Provider.

To be fair, it was in a different era without the understanding we have today in the area of financial support. It was simply not the culture of the day.

By 2000, we had nearly 2 decades of proving God's faithfulness as a family, and seeing His miraculous supply for our itinerant ministry. However, it was time to be stretched again. It is one thing to believe the Lord to supply the needs of your own family and ministry, but it introduces an entirely different level of faith and responsibility when you have to believe Him for the salaries of others.

The Lord began to impress upon our hearts that in order to be more effective in proclaiming the message He had given to us, we would need to start developing a team. As so much of our time was labouring to do administration, we knew that the most critical need was for a personal assistant to relieve us of that task.

Although we had wonderful assistance from one or two volunteers from time to time, we felt it was now time to take the faith step towards our first part-time salaried team member.

As we looked at our financial accounts for the previous six months, it was incredibly clear that we did not have any surplus to pay a salary and yet God had so clearly laid it upon our hearts. Upon further praying it through, we believed the Lord was saying to us to take someone on three days a week and we employed a wonderful personal assistant called Marinda. It is God's faithfulness and mercy that in the process of faith enlargement, He takes us through in stages. Within days of us making that commitment to Marinda, we saw our income increased by the exact amount of her salary.

Marinda was with us for 2 years and her excellence and zeal for the job left us in no doubt that we had passed the point of no return. We were to be 'solo' no more! She was not only an outstanding administrative assistant but she and her husband, Paul, became close friends.

When Marinda was offered a full-time position on staff at CityLife Church (then Waverley Christian Fellowship), we employed a young man called Winston to take her place.

Some months later as the demand of ministry increased, we took him on full-time. Again, the Lord increased our income without any striving on our part.

Our time with Winston was wonderful and his friendship and loyalty was a great strength to Margaret and to me. We remain great friends but the Lord had other things in store for him and he was offered a wonderful opportunity to serve in youth ministry in our then local church, CityLife Church. It was time for us to find a replacement for him.

The Lord began to impress upon my heart that whoever we employed as a PA at this stage of our development, would also have to possess a calling to the prophetic ministry. Although much of the time initially would be spent in administration, there had to be that potential to develop that person into the eventual calling of a prophet. I immediately thought of my son, Steve. At that time he had been full-time as an associate pastor in a local church for approximately 6 years, but I had always believed that he had a prophetic calling on his life.

I shared my heart with Steve and after some time of praying, he came to the conclusion that this was not his time for leaving that particular local church. Although disappointed, I accepted fully the will of God, and began to seek Him as to who it was that He did have in mind.

One day Winston came to see me with a recommendation of his own, named Mark. Mark was involved in various youth leadership roles at CityLife Church and we knew him to be of excellent character. We had an initial interview in which he shared his heart with us, including a prayer goal he had written down some three years before, to be discipled by two men. One of those men was me. After just one interview, Margaret and I knew that we had found someone who was completely our DNA and would fit wonderfully into our ministry team. We hired Mark.

Financially, we were now stretched to the max. Each month was a challenge but God's faithfulness was always there. However, I have lost count of the number of times that the supply came the day before the payment was due. When the accounts were piling up and the clock was ticking, we would look at each other and say, "11:59 again!"

When asking the Lord why this was always so, I felt impressed that it was in order to test our convictions and faith. The pressure to hold our hand out and ask others to help us was often supported by the concern of well-meaning friends but, yet again, we were learning that our convictions are only as strong as the pressures to which they are submitted.

God was speaking again to me very clearly. He told me that although

Mark would eventually become a very fine young prophet, he would not be my personal Elisha nor be the primary one to carry the mantle that had been on my own life. As Margaret and I prayed, we came to the conclusion, once again, that it was our son Steve, but agreed to wait for further confirmation.

When out for coffee with a well-respected prophetic minister from New Zealand, he said that while he had been out walking one day, God had spoken to him and given him a prophetic word for Margaret and I. The word was: *"Your natural son must become your spiritual son and personal Elisha."* Wow! A few days later in our board meeting, one of the board members said the exact same words. So, although Steve had turned us down only a few months earlier and we thought him to be well entrenched in his existing ministry, we agreed to approach him again.

The church in which Steve was the associate minister was going through challenges and he needed to reduce his days from five down to three. He had two options, to either go back to his old secular job part-time or see if I had a couple of days a week work for him. His intention was that this would be temporary until he went back to full-time work at his church.

It was a Thursday afternoon when Margaret and I went to Steve and Sally's home to discuss it. When we sat down, I asked to speak first. I then laid out what I felt and then called Steve to 'leave all and follow his Elisha calling'. I then told him that now was the time to pick up the mantle. I also quoted word for word what he had preached on faith the previous Sunday.

The rest, as they say, is history.

Steve said yes, Sally said yes, his senior minister said yes, the Elders said yes, our friends said yes, his church said yes and that was all by Sunday!!

YOU DID *What?!*

Steve started part-time in August 2006 and came on full-time in November that same year.

Once again, a look at the last six months' accounts revealed that we had been barely breaking even since we had employed Mark. The Lord made it quite clear to me that we were to meet Steve's current salary and not to underpay any of our team members.

We simply did not have the money nor could we see that it could come from anywhere. In the natural, it seemed completely irresponsible to take that step. Again we prayed and again we felt a strong confirmation from the Lord that He had clearly spoken and we were to boldly obey. I should stress here that there was never any doubt of us paying Steve his salary. It was simply another occasion in which Father gave us the privilege of stepping out of our boat at His command.

Upon Steve commencing with us and us going beyond the point of no return, the Lord yet again miraculously provided an increase in our monthly income just prior to Steve's first payday. Obedience first, miracle second!

With so many prophetic types on one team, the Lord in His mercy (and desire for us to actually get something done other than preach!) brought Michelle to us. Michelle is a PA/Executive Assistant with extraordinary abilities. Another step of faith was taken and yet again Father miraculously supplied.

So that I'm not misunderstood, let me share with you the steps I believe are necessary in possessing your future promise:

1. Hear clearly from Father
2. Have it clearly confirmed
3. Allow for the miraculous
4. Make a decision (i.e. don't procrastinate)

5. Have a strong resolve
6. Take your first step

At the time of writing this book we have ten on the team (eight of these on salary). Father is still faithfully providing month by month in ways that constantly amaze us.

I believe God's commission on my life is to raise up at least seven ministers, all with a prophetic heart, plus whatever support roles necessary, by the year 2015. Are we capable of doing such a thing? Of course not, but He most certainly is! And, as Steve has reminded me, that is only the initial goal. His vision for the future of the ministry team is beyond that again.

I am convinced that so many of God's people have not possessed their miraculous intervention for no other reason than that they await the provision before acting in obedience. They want the miracle before the obedience.

YOU DID *What?!*

Chapter Thirty Nine

THE ROAD AHEAD

As I sit here writing this book, I am a 65 year-old grandfather and yet have never felt more fully alive in my entire life.

I believe that the major call upon my life now is to father the next generation and see them emerge to be pure-hearted warriors with a prophetic mantle. It is to see them have the joy and privilege, as I have, of ministering into countless churches, pastors, leaders, movements and nations. I thank God that this is already taking place with our existing team.

YOU DID What?!

Margaret is our specialist on all matters to do with marriage and family, both in ministry material, counselling and being available for those in need. She is also the 'mother' to the team and tirelessly works to keep them healthy mentally and emotionally. With intense prophetic types around, it is Margaret that makes sure we stay normal, reachable and replenished. She is also part of the senior decision-making leadership, comprising of Steve, Margaret and myself.

My son, Steve, is well recognised now as a prophet and his ministry is gaining momentum both here and overseas. He also speaks into the lives of a growing number of pastors. His "Believing in You" daily devotional email is read by thousands around the world and has recently been released as a 365 day devotional book. He is now the "Executive Director" member of the team, in as much as he takes the dreams and journeys them to reality. He oversees the team on all matters other than vision, ministry expression and policy, and is a huge part of why we have grown in recent years.

Helen has a powerful ability to activate the gifts of God in people and is a gifted prophetic communicator, preacher and writer. Her "Enliven Blog" is a weekly teaching on spiritual gifts and how we can function in them in a God-honouring and people-honouring way. This was read by over 23,000 people in 2012 alone.

Clayton has an earned Doctorate from Wheaton College, USA and is an outstanding theologian with a passionate, prophetic heart and a great teaching gift.

Malcolm (Helen's husband) not only ministers prophetically very effectively with Helen, but has a wonderful gift of exhortation. His buoyant faith and constant encouragement of others have made him our "Roving Ambassador".

Mark, another of our full-time team for the last six years, has now gone back into the marketplace for a season. He has emerged as an excellent young prophet, and spoke into the lives of youth groups and churches.

Michelle is our Personal Assistant extraordinaire who constantly works miracles to ensure we all stay sane. So much of what is now being achieved is due to her dedication and excellence.

Kamal has a wonderful prophetic gift, ministers well from the Word, and currently plays a vital role in our resource development.

Carmen is our bookkeeper and has such an awesome and beautiful spirit.

Anne helps with resources, administration, cleaning and powerful prayer. She always spreads joy and serves with such passion.

The team's ministry in the preaching of the Word is receiving excellent feedback and results. Churches are significantly impacted by a timely 'now' word ministered with passion and authority. The feedback I have received has been quite remarkable in regard to the detail and accuracy of the prophetic words that they bring with life changing results in individuals and churches. Very rarely have I heard of ministry so consistent at such a level. They have also ministered in prophetic presbyteries to pastors and to leadership groups.

As a team, we are now ministering into the lives of many thousands of people every year.

There are seminars, pastors' conferences, ministering into large apostolically-led local churches and the smallest of rural churches. There is the mentoring of pastors and the development of 'sons' and 'daughters' as the emerging apostolic generation. There are the many hours of counseling pastors and leaders on both personal and ministerial issues. There is the speaking into marketplace ministries, including to boards of significant businesses in the nation. There is the communication of the Word through books, DVDs, CDs, website and emails in obedience to our commission to 'greatly multiply the seed'. There is the resourcing of missionaries in Australia with the Aboriginal people and those serving in nations around the world. There is the sending forth of members of our own team to those nations. There is the wide open door of Europe where pastors and leaders have reached out to us with a hungry heart.

And this is just the beginning. Our team now totals ten including two who come in one day a week. I know that God will continue to add many 'sons' and 'daughters' in the years ahead.

The Lord has also given us a clear vision to see a property established which will be a home base for the increased ministry team and to accommodate the teaching aspect of their ministries. Such a property is also to become a place of refuge for pastors and leaders who have become weary or wounded in the fight. We see it as a place of replenishment and restoration.

We call it 'Antioch' -

- The Empowered Life School: A training and releasing centre for those who want to live the empowered Christian life as well as empowering courses for ministers.

- The Life Replenishment Retreat: A place of healing, replenishment and re-igniting for those in ministry [Church and Marketplace] who need a fresh touch from God and some prophetic insight.

- David McCracken Ministries: A ministry base for the DMM team.

We have more nations opening up to us than ever before and, by God's grace, our acceptance and credibility in the Body of Christ has never been stronger.

When I look at the past, I am overwhelmed with gratitude. When

I look at the future, I marvel at the hope that lies before us. I have often joked that I will have to live until I am 105 to accomplish the dreams God has placed in my heart. It is going to be an awesome ride and I look forward to sharing it with you a decade or so from now.

Let me close with some of my opening statements concerning my motivation for writing this book.

... to bring the reader to a place of being overawed by the wonder, love, faithfulness, forgiveness, long-suffering, generosity, power and sovereignty of my Father!

I want people to have a hunger to know Him more, trust Him more, obey Him more, worship Him more, love Him more, and walk in greater intimacy with His heart as a result of reading this book. My one objective is that you may know Him as I do, love Him as I do, and serve Him passionately with total abandonment. And that you may be aided to do so as you read of His amazing grace in the life of one sinner who was, and is, in human terms, so completely ordinary.

Friends, Father takes delight in doing extraordinary things through very ordinary people. Let me encourage you to dare to live a life of abandoned devotion and service to Him, and to walk with confidence into the life of indescribable love and adventure that He has planned for you.

This will have to be it for now. In a while, when there are more stories of tears and laughter to be told, we will fellowship again. Life is a journey, and I thank you for letting me share a little of mine with you.

In gratitude for yesterday and anticipation of tomorrow,

David

OTHER RESOURCES BY DAVID McCRACKEN MINISTRIES

At David McCracken Ministries, we have a growing team of prophetic and teaching ministers. Following are some of the resources from the team that will empower you. You can view and purchase these and other resources from our online store at www.davidmccracken.securestore.com.au.

David McCracken:
An Incorruptible Heart

God is searching for those in whom He can safely entrust the authority of His Kingdom and the mantle of leadership and influence within that Kingdom. Rather than greatness of stature, God is looking for greatness of integrity, devotion and humility. An Incorruptible Heart addresses the vital elements that we must all endeavour to pursue if finishing well is our goal. An incorruptible heart is possible for you, and possessing it will empower your future success for God's glory!

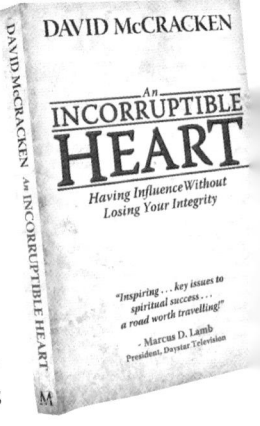

More from David McCracken:
Pages of Empowerment – Volumes 1 to 5

Overcomers: Born to Rule (DVD & CD)

The Marriage Journey (DVD)

Leaders of Destiny (DVD)

God's Emerging Prophets (CD)

Steve McCracken:
Believing in You – Volume 1

Helen Calder:
Growing Your Prophetic and Prayer Gifts

How to be a Supernatural Christian in Your Everyday World

Pray for the Lost

Prophetic People in a Changing Church

Unlocking the Gift of Discernment

Visit our website for free resources (articles, sermons, blogs, etc.)
and more information.
www. davidmccracken.org